THE SUFFICIENCY AND DEFECTS

OF THE

ENGLISH COMMUNION OFFICE

THE SUFFICIENCY AND DEFECTS

OF THE

ENGLISH COMMUNION OFFICE

by

A. G. WALPOLE SAYER, B.D.

Vicar of Henlow and former Exhibitioner of
Pembroke College, Cambridge

Cambridge

at the University Press

1911

CAMBRIDGE UNIVERSITY PRESS
Cambridge, New York, Melbourne, Madrid, Cape Town,
Singapore, São Paulo, Delhi, Mexico City

Cambridge University Press
The Edinburgh Building, Cambridge CB2 8RU, UK

Published in the United States of America by Cambridge University Press, New York

www.cambridge.org
Information on this title: www.cambridge.org/9781107646254

First published 1911
First paperback edition 2013

A catalogue record for this publication is available from the British Library

ISBN 978-1-107-64625-4 Paperback

PREFACE

THE object which led to the enterprise of this subject was essentially practical. Considerable outcry had been raised against the interpolation into the service by the Celebrant of parts of the Unreformed Office. The outcry interpreted this action as throwing doubt or discredit on the Office of our Church. And this interpretation is justified by the open avowals of many who are addicted to this practice. They allege defect or deficiency in our Office. Others, indeed, without such allegation or conscious admission, defend their interpolations as conducing to greater fulness or richness.

The object of this work in part is to attempt to disprove the charges of insufficiency and to show the redundancy of such interpolations. The nature of the interpolations in view has been already defined. There is no reference to any private[1] intercessions or devotions of the Celebrant, but to the direct interpolation of portions of other Offices.

On the other hand, in contrast with this deprecia-tion of our Office, intentional or not, there is present

---

[1] Which indeed were recognised in a Rubric of the Armenian Rite, just before the Priest's Communion. Brightman, *Liturgies Eastern and Western*, Vol. I. p. 451.

amongst us an opposite tendency. This is to declaim on our "incomparable Liturgy," to deprecate any need or possibility of improvement and to discover various fanciful interpretations of its present structure.

With this in mind, the writer's object is to indicate defects and needs of amendment in our Office, while defending it from charges of insufficiency.

Attention will be confined to the Canon as the essential part of the Office.

The method pursued will be, to examine first the Scripture narratives and the older Liturgies, in order to gain an idea of the requisite structure and composition of the Office. Having done this, we shall review the English Office of 1549 and go on to the comparison of our Office with the idea so gained. And after this, subsequent chapters will deal with the various points, which such a comparison shows requiring consideration.

The writer is under a general obligation to very many works bearing directly and indirectly on the subject.

In particular he is indebted to Mr Brightman's *Liturgies Eastern and Western*, Vol. I.; Mgr. Duchesne's *Christian Worship* in the S.P.C.K. translation; Bishop Dowden's *Annotated Scottish Communion Office* and the article on "Alms and Oblations" in *Further Studies in the Prayer Book* by the same writer; Mr Darwell Stone's *History of the Doctrine of the Eucharist*; Bishop Drury on "Elevation"; and Mr Bishop's Appendix to Dom Connolly's edition of the *Homilies of Narsai*.

The passage on "Anamnesis" was, however, all done

before reading Mr Stone's book, likewise Appendix C, before the writer saw Messrs Gasquet and Bishop's book on *Edward VI and the Book of Common Prayer* ; and the view of the meaning of the phrase " Holy Spirit and Word " in the 1549 book and of the reason for its omission was taken without any conscious reference to Bishop Dowden's *Workmanship of the Prayer Book.*

In conclusion it is but due to gratefully acknowledge several kind suggestions and criticisms of the Divinity Professors of the University of Cambridge, the courtesy and care of the staff of the University Press, and the kind help of a young friend in the preparation of the Index.

A. G. W. S.

October, 1911

CONTENTS

CHAPTER I

THE SCRIPTURE NARRATIVES

§ 1.   IN examining the narratives of the Institution, we find that two words are employed for what the Master did and said with regard to the Bread and Wine.

SS. Matthew (xxvi. 26 sq.) and Mark (xiv. 22 sq.) say that He "blessed" (εὐλογήσας) the Bread and "gave thanks" (εὐχαριστήσας) over the Cup.

Εὐλογέω signifies the speaking of a word for good, the invocation of good upon a person or thing, a calling on God to do well unto a person or thing and bestow some gift upon them.

Εὐχαριστέω universally signifies in the N.T. "to give thanks," to express thanks for gifts.   And when addressed to GOD, there is involved, in such εὐχαριστία, the additional idea of worship and humble adoration.

The words therefore connote two different, though allied, ideas.   And the narratives of SS. Matthew and Mark alone would seem to suggest that the Lord invoked the Divine Benedictory Power on the Bread and not upon the Cup and that for the Cup He gave thanks as for a gift from GOD and not for the Bread.

But there are two further narratives of the Institution. SS. Luke (xxii. 17 sq.) and Paul (1 Cor. xi. 23 sq.) say that He "gave thanks" (εὐχαριστήσας) over the Bread and by the word "likewise" (ὡσαύτως) imply the same word with regard to the Cup. They make no mention of any "blessing" of either. Yet we know that they were describing the same event as SS. Matthew and Mark. In fact they only exhibit the well-known variation as to details which marks the narratives of the same occurrence by different writers. They are indeed complementary to one another.

As we read the two forms of the narrative together, we certainly conclude that the Lord both "blessed" (εὐλογήσας) the Bread and "gave thanks" over it (εὐχαριστήσας). And both accounts agree in mentioning the "giving of thanks" over the Cup.

Yet S. Paul speaks in the previous chapter (x. 16) of his First Epistle to the Corinthians, in which his narrative of the Institution is found, of "the Cup of blessing which we bless" (τὸ ποτήριον τῆς εὐλογίας ὃ εὐλογοῦμεν). The identity of this Cup is clear from his interrogation concerning it: viz. "Is it not the Communion of the BLOOD of Christ?" He therefore used a form of "blessing" over the Cup, which he would never have done, unless he had known that the Lord "blessed the Cup" as well as "gave thanks" over it.

We therefore conclude that the Lord made use of

an expression of "benediction" as well as of "thanks-giving" over the Cup, as He did over the Bread. And we further gather that every Communion Office must likewise have a form of "benediction" or "prayer that GOD will bless it into a heavenly good" (Evans, in *Speaker's Commentary in loc.*); and a form of thanks-giving and adoration to GOD for His goodness.

And as to the form and manner of this Benediction, we recall the significance of the word εὐλογέω etymo-logically. It is to call upon GOD to do well unto, by bestowing some heavenly gift. And that this is how S. Paul understood the term is clear from what he says, "the Cup of blessing which we bless, is it not the Communion of the Blood of Christ?"

The word Communion (κοινωνία) never signifies in the N.T. participation but fellowship and that with persons. The genitive is not therefore possessive but signifies the source of the Communion. The Cup of blessing which we bless is the (means of Communion with GOD and man) Communion which springs from the BLOOD of Christ.

This indicates that some spiritual quality has been conferred by the "Blessing" on what was before but common wine. This could only be by the Power of GOD. And it would suggest that the "Blessing" in-cluded and should always include an Invocation of GOD's Power, either in direct or indirect terms.

And then as we reflect on the force of S. Paul's statement about the Cup of Blessing and the Bread broken and his conclusion that "he that receiveth

unworthily is guilty of the Body and Blood of the Lord"
(1 Cor. xi. 27)—we cannot but feel the necessity of
humble acknowledgement of unworthiness to receive
" Food so awful and so sweet" and of prayer for right
disposition and grace to receive "worthily" and with
profit. Some devotions for Preparation of the Communicants should accordingly find a place in any Communion
Office. Likewise, the Receiving of so great a Gift should
be followed by " Thanks to GOD for His unspeakable
Gift."

§ 2.   As we turn again to the narratives of Institution, we find that SS. Luke (xxii. 19) and Paul (1 Cor.
xi. 24, 25) record that the Lord said, " Do this in
remembrance of Me" (τοῦτο ποιεῖτε εἰς τὴν ἐμὴν
ἀνάμνησιν).

S. Luke makes the words follow " This is My BODY
which is given for you " (τοῦτό ἐστι τὸ σῶμά μου τὸ
ὑπὲρ ὑμῶν διδόμενον) and probably implies them after
the words said over the Cup by the " Likewise " with
which he introduces them. (Assuming this second
reference to the Cup in his Gospel to be his.)

S. Paul records the words after the mention of both
the Bread and the Cup.

Do this.

S. Luke, like S. Paul, omits the words " Take, eat "
before " This is My BODY," thus leaving " This do "
alone and without indication of its meaning.

So S. Paul reads, " this is My BLOOD ; Do this," etc.

Very many have interpreted this in a sacrificial sense,
viz. " Offer this."   And it is quite true that a whole

catena of passages from the LXX may be adduced for the use of ποιέω in that sense. In fact there are 60 or 80 instances.

Sometimes it is used absolutely alone, as here, e.g. 1 Kings (in LXX 3 Kings) xi. 33 ἐποίησεν τῇ 'Ἀστάρτῃ, 2 Kings (in LXX 4 Kings) xvii. 32 ἐποίησαν ἑαυτοῖς ἐν οἴκῳ τῶν ὑψηλῶν, Job xlii. 8 ποιήσει κάρπωσιν, though in the second case there had been a mention of " making of priests " and in the third of the " taking of animals," which may be taken as some clue to the sense. Count-less cases there are of its use in a sacrificial context. But there is no instance of this sacrificial sense in the N.T. except with remote possibility in S. Luke ii. 27 ποιῆσαι...περὶ αὐτοῦ (A.V. " to do for Him "). There is practically no evidence of the Greek and Latin Fathers so understanding the words[1]. They took them in the ordinary meaning of " perform this action." And the early Liturgies never used ποιεῖν but προσφέρειν in the Oblation.

And in fact the sacrificial interpretation has arisen from forgetting the complementary harmony of the accounts and the natural bearing of the context. The command "Take, eat" is not excluded by S. Luke's omission. It must be brought in for the full idea of the Institution. And, brought in, it indicates the

[1] Justin, *Trypho* 41, does seem to so use the word, τοῦ ἄρτου τῆς εὐχαριστίας ὃν...'Ἰησοῦς Χριστὸς παρέδωκε ποιεῖν.

In the Liturgy of S. Chrysostom as now used, in the Preparatory Service before the Service begins at the Altar the Deacon says to the Priest, Καιρὸς τοῦ ποιῆσαι τῷ Κυρίῳ. (Brightman, *Liturgies Eastern and Western*, Vol. I. p. 362.)

6 THE SCRIPTURE NARRATIVES

meaning of τοῦτο ποιεῖτε, viz. λάβετε, φάγετε, τοῦτό
ἐστι τὸ σῶμά μου, τοῦτο ποιεῖτε κτλ. Do this, viz.
take, eat.

And this interpretation finds support, I submit, from
S. Paul's narrative. He agrees with S. Luke in the
account of the Consecration of the Bread, but he re-
peats τοῦτο ποιεῖτε in connection with the Consecration
of the Cup, with added words which give a key to the
sense, viz. τοῦτο ποιεῖτε, ὁσάκις ἐὰν πίνητε.

Further the words followed not only the Command
to Receive, but the Blessing, the Giving of Thanks, the
Breaking of the Bread, and the Delivery.

" Do this " means, therefore, I venture to think—do
all which I have done, Bless, Give thanks, Break, Deliver, as well as, do what I am commanding you to do—
Receive.

The words are, on this assumption, non-significant,
except as suggesting a close imitation of the Institution
in each Office.

§ 3. The Lord then added—εἰς τὴν ἐμὴν ἀνάμνησιν.
For the interpretation of this, the Harmony of the
Gospel accounts supplies no assistance. The *exact
formula* occurs twice in the Old Testament.

In Lev. xxiv. 7 it is defined as προκείμενα τῷ
Κυρίῳ—of the incense and salt placed on the shew-bread.

In Numbers x. 10 σαλπιεῖτε...ἐπὶ ταῖς θυσίαις...καὶ
ἔσται ὑμῖν ἀνάμνησις ἔναντι τοῦ θεοῦ (" ut sint vobis in
recordationem Dei vestri," Vg.).

In both of these plainly it is the reminding of GOD
that is in view.

Also in the Titles of Psalms[1] xxxvii. and lxix. the same form occurs representing the Hebrew לְהַזְכִּיר which according to Gesenius (Lexicon) requires an object, other than self, being Hiphil, and implies GOD as the object. (The same Hebrew occurs in Gen. xl. 14 " bring me to remembrance before Pharaoh.")

The *idea* is of frequent occurrence, expressed by derivatives of the same Hebrew root and by Greek cognates of ἀνάμνησις.

In Exodus xxviii. 12 the two stones engraved with the names of the Twelve Tribes are ordered to be worn on the shoulders of the Ephod " for a memorial." " Aaron shall bear their names before the Lord on his shoulders for a memorial " (Heb. לְזִכָּרֹן, as in Numbers x. 10 where LXX has ἀνάμνησις).

And the Lord's use of the words on that occasion would certainly recall the application of the idea to the Passover at its institution: Exodus xii. 14 reads:

καὶ ἔσται ἡ ἡμέρα ὑμῖν αὕτη μνημόσυνον (לְזִכָּרֹן) καὶ ἑορτάσετε αὐτὴν ἑορτὴν κυρίῳ κτλ.

The Festival was to be a memorial to them, it is there to bring to their mind the great mercy of GOD. But it was also " for the Lord "—to be an offering of praise to GOD and a reminder to Him of His goodness as a ground and plea for further mercies.

And μνημόσυνον (for אַזְכָּרָה) occurs in Isaiah lxvi. 3, Lev. ii. 2, 9, 16, v. 12, Numbers v. 26, to signify a memorial offering which calls to GOD's Mind.

---

[1] In Hebrew xxxviii. and lxx.

It was the name of that part of the Minchah which was burned with frankincense on the altar; the sweet savour of which ascending to heaven was ordained to signify the commending to GOD of the remembrance of the worshipper.

And this brings to notice the other use of ἀνά-μνησις in Hebrews x. 3, viz. ἀνάμνησις ἁμαρτιῶν, which recalls Numbers v. 15 θυσία μνημοσύνου, ἀναμιμνή-σκουσα ἁμαρτίαν.

There is a bringing of sin to mind, but the connection with θυσία μνημοσύνου shows that it was to GOD's Mind that the remembrance was brought to plead for mercy and forgiveness.

Bearing in mind, then, the use of the actual words in the Old Testament, the constant use of the idea of memorial in a technical sense in their Scriptures and in their religion at that day, there can be but little doubt that there is strong ground for the conclusion that the Lord meant by His charge ("Do this as a remembrance of Me") that this Service was to be a Memorial of Him to GOD. It would remind them of His saving work, but it was chiefly and primarily to remind GOD of it for man's continual benefit.

So Bishop Wren, in a paper of suggestions for Prayer Book Revision, proposed to add in the Consecration Prayer at the "narrative of Institution," "for a remembrance of Him by showing His Death and Passion," and of this writes:

"This would be thus, first, because S. Paul's word is καταγγέλλετε, 1 Cor. xi. 26; and secondly, because εἰς τὴν ἐμὴν ἀνάμνησιν being spoken by Christ does most properly signify, To put Me in mind of you; Christ of us and not us in mind of Christ."

And the same view of the words is taken by Bishop Bull (in *The Corruptions of the Church of Rome*, Section iii.), "They (the Romans) held the Eucharist to be a Commemorative Sacrifice and so do we... according to Our Saviour's words when He ordained this holy rite, 'Do this in commemoration of Me.'"

Hence we should expect in the Office a verbal commemoration of "the Sacrifice of the Death of Christ" and of His Command and Institution. We should expect a pleading in definite words of His Life and Death. We should expect prayer that His Sacrifice may be accepted for us to our benefit. And in a public Office we should also expect a general prayer particularising benefits desired—with definite supplications and intercessions for definite persons and for definite needs—for the congregation, the whole Church and for all men—together with thanksgivings of a similar definite reference.

And as the Service is an Offering, according to the conclusions at which we have arrived, reasonable reflection would also desiderate a prayer in the Office for the acceptance of the actual material elements used in the Service as symbols and media of the Real Offering.

As a result, therefore, of our investigations and reflections, we may conclude that essential in our Communion Office are:

1. Expressions of Thanksgiving and Adoration.

2. Benedictory prayer, including a direct Invocation of Divine Power to fit the Elements for their purpose.

3. Verbal Commemoration of Christ's Sacrifice and Institution.

4. Verbal Oblation of the Memorial.

5. Intercessions and Thanksgivings offered along with and through the Great Oblation.

Besides there are as reasonable requisites:

6. An offering of the Elements, in a solemn act and with suitable words.

7. Prayers for pardon, acceptance and worthy participation.

8. Also thanksgiving after Receiving so great a Gift is dictated by a sense of the fitness of things[1].

---

[1] In Acts xx. we read of a Sermon at the "Breaking of Bread" and in the Colossian Epistle a direction for a Lection—which shows Preaching and Lections as desirable adjuncts of a Service of Celebration of the Divine Mysteries.

CHAPTER II

EARLY REFERENCES AND ACCOUNTS

WHEN we leave the pages of Scripture, we are beset with the difficulty which confronts all students of the early history of the Church, viz. the absence of early documents.

This is due, in part, to the reserve which shrank from committing their sacred rites or beliefs to writing and so putting them in the reach of those outside; and in part also to the large destruction of such sacred books as were in existence, in the persecutions. We have therefore no complete specimen of a Communion Office earlier than the fourth century. And early references to the Office are few.

In the earliest days, indeed, it may be, there was, with a settled outline, liberty for extempore forms of expression—especially in the "thanksgiving." The Didache (§ 10) in fact says "The Prophets permit to give thanks as much as they wish." And Justin gives an indication of the continuance of the same state of things, when he says, describing the Service in his first *Apology* (presented to Antoninus Pius A.D. 139), "the

President...taking the Bread and Wine...offers thanks at considerable length " (c. LXV. § 3), and again, " the President offers prayers and thanksgivings with all his might " (c. LXVII. § 5).

I.   First, various isolated allusions.

The *primitive form of consecration* may be assumed to be a prayer, i.e. a supplication and not a mere narration of the words of Institution. For Origen (*c. Celsum* VIII. p. 33) says, " we, giving thanks to the Maker of the Universe, eat also, with prayer and thanksgiving for blessings received, our oblations of bread, which because of the *prayer* (διὰ τὴν εὐχὴν) becomes a certain holy Body." And this prayer, indicated in these general terms, may well have, always or frequently, taken the form of an Invocation of GOD (ἐπίκλησις τοῦ θεοῦ). For Irenaeus writes (*c. Haer.* lib. IV. c. 18 and X. c. 18), " the Bread...after receiving the invocation of GOD upon it, is no longer common bread, but the Eucharist."

At the same time Tertullian says that our Lord " took bread...and made it His Body by saying ' This is my body...' " (*Adv. Marc.* IV. 40).

In all probability therefore the primitive form of Consecration included some sort of Prayer over the Elements imploring GOD'S grace upon them, and the narrative of Institution—both being regarded as necessary and efficacious for the Consecration.

The primitive Eucharists, also, *contained intercessions and not only for the living but for the departed.* Arnobius (*Adv. Gentes* lib. IV. cap. 36, *P. L.* V. 1076), referring to the destruction of Churches, says, " What have our conventicles done that they should be ruthlessly destroyed, places in which GOD Most High is prayed to, peace and pardon are asked for all men...for persons still living and for persons delivered from the bondage of the flesh ? "

Tertullian (*De Cor.* 3) says, " We offer oblations for the dead on the anniversary of their birth."

Origen (lib. III. in Job, tom. ii. p. 902, col. i.), " we devoutly make memorial of thy Saints and of our parents and friends, who die in the faith."

It is true in the last three there is only the general "use" of the term memorial and oblation and mysteries to connect the Intercession with the Eucharist. But that general " use " is well known and established.

S. Cyprian[1] however definitely testifies to established practice.—Speaking of one who nominated a Cleric as executor, he says : " that man does not deserve to be named at the Altar in the prayer of the Priests, who was ready to call away priests and ministers from the Altar." And he goes on to speak of this prayer for the departed as a " deprecatio "—a term used in a like sense in the Gallican Churches.

II. When we come to early accounts of the Office, we must first consider that in the Didache, an ancient document of uncertain origin, but of the early 2nd century, which gives some longer reference to the Eucharist, and from which I have already quoted a remark about the prophets' liberty of extemporary thanksgiving.

[1] Ep. LXVI. p. 114.

In chapter XIV. it says, "On the Lord's day gather yourselves together and break bread and give thanks, first confessing your transgressions, that your sacrifice may be pure."

Here is only an indication of confession of sin as a preparation, followed by a ceremonial breaking of bread, and thanksgiving either accompanying or following the breaking of bread.

But in chapters IX. and X. there is a longer account of the Eucharistic Thanksgiving: "As to the Eucharist, give ye thanks on this wise. First for the cup: 'We thank Thee, Our Father, for the Holy Vine of David Thy Servant; which Thou hast made known to us by Jesus Thy Servant. *Thine is the Glory for evermore.*' For the broken bread: 'We thank Thee, Our Father, for the life and the knowledge which Thou hast made known to us by Jesus Thy Servant. *Thine is the Glory for evermore.* As this broken bread, scattered on the mountains, was brought into a single whole, may Thy Church in like manner be gathered together from the ends of the Earth into Thy kingdom, for *Thine is the Glory and the Power, through Jesus Christ, for evermore.*' Let no man eat or drink of your Eucharist but they who are baptised in the Name of the Lord, for it was of this the Lord said, 'give not that which is holy to dogs.'

"After you are satisfied thus give thanks ($\epsilon \dot{v} \chi \alpha \rho \iota$-$\sigma \tau \dot{\eta} \sigma \alpha \tau \epsilon$): We thank Thee, Holy Father, for thy Holy Name, which Thou hast made to dwell in our hearts, for the knowledge, faith and immortality which Thou hast revealed to us through Jesus Thy Servant. *Thine is the Glory for evermore.*

" It is Thou, Almighty Lord, who hast created the universe for the glory of Thy Name, and hast given to men meat and drink for enjoyment, that they may give Thee thanks. But to us Thou hast given spiritual meat and drink and life eternal through Thy Servant. We give Thee thanks before everything because Thou art mighty. *Thine is the Glory for evermore.*

" Be mindful, Lord, of Thy Church, to deliver it from all evil, and to grant it perfection in Thy love. Gather it together from the four winds of heaven, this Church that is sanctified for the kingdom which Thou hast prepared for it, for *Thine is the Power and Glory for evermore.* May grace come and this world pass away ! Hosanna to the Son of David ! If any one is holy let him come; if any one is not let him repent. Maran atha. Amen.

" But the prophets permit to give thanks as much as they wish."

All this is vague and difficult to interpret.

" *After you are satisfied*[1] " seems to some to signify the actual satisfying of hunger in the social and religious meal—the Agape—with which as a preliminary, in the earliest days, the Actual Eucharist was incorporated. This would indicate that the references prior to this were forms of grace over actual food consumed, succeeded by a reminder of the requisites for the Solemn Sacrament to follow.

[1] μετὰ τὸ ἐμπλησθῆναι.

And it would make cap. x. a description of the Eucharist proper—consisting of Eucharistic Act, General Supplication, Solemn Warning—to be followed by Reception.

In support of this contention, it is urged that (1) there is reference to "satisfaction" in the Agape elsewhere, e.g. Canons of Hippolytus 172–8 "Edant bibantque ad satietatem...in divina praesentia cum laude Dei," and Tertullian (*Apol.* cap. XXXIX. "Ita saturantur, ut qui meminerint etiam per noctem adorandum Deum sibi esse"); (2) the cup precedes the bread; (3) such forms as those in cap. IX. are without parallel in known Eucharistic Offices; (4) there is a separate and distinct reference to "the breaking of bread and giving of thanks" later in cap. XIV.

But the question is, whether this method of interpretation is not dictated by the desire to interpret in accordance with later usage. The position of the cup first may be but an instance of early unsettled usage, and has certainly parallels in S. Luke's account of the Institution xxii. 17 and in the references of S. Paul in 1 Cor. x. 16.

The uniqueness of the Thanksgiving of cap. IX., if Eucharistic, is really no argument. The later reference is only a further order as to frequency of Communion and cannot be taken to rule out a passage like cap. IX. which begins περὶ δὲ τῆς εὐχαριστίας.

We must try and take the passage as it stands and let it speak for itself.

The recurring ascription surely shows the unity of

chapters IX. and X. as together describing a single entity.

The terms of reference in the thanksgivings of c. IX. have not the slightest bearing on actual food, but solely on spiritual grace—refreshment and life conveyed to men through the sacramental bread and wine. And indeed κλάσμα seems incapable of association with anything but the Bread Broken in the Eucharist.

While the Thanksgiving at the opening of c. X. after μετὰ δὲ τὸ ἐμπλησθῆναι is for "Thy holy Name which Thou hast made to dwell in our hearts." By themselves these words might mean merely the knowledge of GOD, but following on μετὰ τὸ ἐμπλησθῆναι, it is difficult to avoid associating the "indwelling" with the "satisfying" and "the Name" with Sacramental Gifts.

Therefore, I venture to submit that the whole account (both c. IX. and c. X.) must be taken of the Eucharist.

The Agape was indeed, in those early days, joined with the Eucharist proper, but the forms here seem incapable of reference to anything but the Eucharist. τὸ ἐμπλησθῆναι, then, refers to Communion. There is a metaphorical use of the word likewise, in Rom. xv. 2, of the refreshment and satisfaction derivable from earthly fellowship. And this interpretation finds support from the fact that the version of this same narrative given in the Apostolic Constitutions VII. 9 and 10, paraphrases μετὰ τὸ ἐμπλησθῆναι by μετὰ δὲ τὴν μετάληψιν—which shows that the compiler understood these words of Communicating.

There is indeed no mention of the use of the Narrative of Institution, or of any prayer over the Elements. But the thanksgiving over Cup and Bread may well be taken to regard the Consecration as effected, and the Bread is spoken of as bread already broken.

What we seem to have then in these chapters is:

(1) (Implication of Consecration.)

(2) Thanksgiving for Cup and Broken Bread.

(3) Prayer for Unity.

(4) A Solemn Warning—excluding the unbaptised from Reception and proclaiming the necessity for holiness. This may—in part—represent the subsequently regular τὰ ἅγια τοῖς ἁγίοις before Communion.

(5) Communicants' preparation implied in the reminder of the need of holiness.

(6) Communion.

After Communion:

(7) Thanks for Sacramental Indwelling (Thanksgiving after Reception).

(8) Thanks for Creation, Food and Spiritual Nourishment.

(9) Prayer for the Preservation, Perfection and Unity of the Church and its entrance into Glory.

(10) Prayer for the coming of Grace and the End.

(11) Another solemn warning about Communion.

[This last, those who interpret c. IX. of the Agape make the equivalent to τὰ ἅγια τοῖς ἁγίοις and the prelude to Communion. But the reference to Baptism, in the first warning of c. IX., as a requisite for Reception, may well imply the continued presence of

Catechumens (in later days sent away.). Then this second warning at the end may be taken for an appeal to them (present, but not having been able to receive) to put themselves in a position to Receive—by repentance and Baptism.]

This seems, on the whole, the best interpretation of a difficult account.

There is a double Thanksgiving

(1) before or at Consecration;

(2) after Communion.

There is a double Intercession, before and after Communion.

III. *Justin's account* must next be considered.

Justin in fact gives two accounts, one of the celebrations following a Baptism, in chap. LXV. of his first *Apology*; the other in chap. LXVII. of the usual Sunday celebration, which begins in a more detailed manner and then concludes briefly after referring back to the former account. The two are complementary.

Chap. LXVII.: "On the day which is called Sunday, an Assembly is made...and *the Memoirs of the Apostles* and the writings of the prophets are read as time permits.

"Then, when the Reader stops, he who presides (ὁ προεστὼς) makes an *Admonition....* Afterwards, we all arise and utter *prayers* and as I said before (chap. LXV.) when we cease praying, *bread and wine and water are brought*" (προσφέρεται), and he who presides likewise sends up *prayers* and *thanksgivings*, to the best of his ability...."

Chap. LXV. : "and he taking it sends up *praise and glory* (αἶνον καὶ δόξαν) to the Father of all, through the Name of the Son and of the Holy Spirit. And he makes at great length *thanksgiving* (εὐχαριστίαν) for that we have been counted worthy to receive these Gifts from Him (GOD). And when he finishes the *prayers* and *thanksgivings*, all the people present respond 'Amen.'...And when the President has given thanks (εὐχαριστήσαντος) and all the people responded, those who are called Deacons among us *give to each of those present* to partake of the bread and wine and water over which thanks has been given (εὐχαριστηθέντος) and to the absent they carry It away."

Now there are several points that claim attention in this.

(i) In the account of the Sunday Service in chap. LXVII. he mentions "prayers" after the Offertory (bread, etc., προσφέρεται[1]) as well as before: "Prayers and thanksgivings," he says. This can hardly be an equivalent for αἶνον καὶ δόξαν in the former narrative: he had only just used εὐχὰς of "prayers" and would not be likely to employ it again in a different sense. We

---

[1] In the Testament of Our Lord II. 10 the phrase "to offer the oblation" is used of the Deacon's bringing the Elements to the Celebrant at the Offertory. And in the Canons of Hippolytus XIX. 14 "Deinde Diaconus incipit sacrificare."

This rather points to what was probably the earliest idea, that the Offering of the Memorial took place with the bringing of the Elements at the Offertory. This would account for the connection of the Intercessions with the Offertory. (See p. 47 note.)

cannot avoid the conclusion, therefore, that prayers followed as well as preceded the Offertory.

(ii)   Before the Offertory he says, " *We* arise and utter prayers," and after the Offertory, " The *President* utters prayers likewise," i.e. just as the congregation did before. The former were joined in by the congregation, the latter said by the " President " alone.

(iii)   In the account in chap. LXV. he describes these prayers before the Offertory as " united (κοινὰς) "—for we read, " We lead him (the newly baptised) to where they are gathered together, who are about to make united (κοινὰς) prayers for themselves and for him... and for all others everywhere. Ceasing from our prayers, we salute one another with a kiss. Then bread and wine and water, etc." (κοινὰς) " united " denotes their congregational character. This supports the conclusion already drawn from the other account. We also see the all-embracing scope of these intercessions.

They were probably set forms after the style of a Litany in which the people joined.

(iv)   In the account of chap. LXVII. he says that " The President utters prayers and thanksgivings to the best of his ability (ὅση δύναμις αὐτῷ)." This indicates at any rate scope for extemporary effort, even if some framework was settled.

Justin also (*Ap.* I. LXVI.) tells something of the *manner of Consecration*: οὕτως καὶ τὴν δι᾽ εὐχῆς λόγου τοῦ παρ᾽ αὐτοῦ εὐχαριστηθεῖσαν τροφήν.

The phrase is difficult. It may mean " praying the form of words which came from Him "—i.e. the Lord's

Prayer or some other prayer which the Lord taught His Apostles. On this Bp Drury (*Elevation*, p. 14) says, "the tradition that the Apostles used the Lord's Prayer alone would suitably interpret his words."

But this ignores the context. The sentence is the second member of a comparison and its interpretation is thus indicated with reasonable certainty. The whole runs: ὃν τρόπον διὰ λόγου θεοῦ σαρκοποιηθεὶς 'Ιησοῦς Χριστὸς...οὕτως καὶ τὴν δι' εὐχῆς λόγου τοῦ παρ' αὐτοῦ κτλ.

Evidently the meaning is that the Consecration is effected by prayer for the same power, by which the Incarnation itself was effected. What power does he intend by Λόγος? The answer is in chap. XXXIII. of the same *Apology*. Commenting on S. Luke i. 35 he says: τὸ πνεῦμα οὖν καὶ τὴν δύναμιν τὴν παρὰ τοῦ θεοῦ οὐδὲν ἄλλο νοῆσαι θέμις ἢ τὸν Λόγον, ὃς καὶ πρωτότοκος τῷ θεῷ ἐστι. It is hardly necessary in a work on the present subject to dwell on the way in which this is to be reconciled with the Gospel Narrative of the Lord's Conception—suffice it to point out that S. Luke prefixed no Article to πνεῦμα. At any rate, Justin gave it as his deliberate interpretation, that the Incarnation was effected by the personal action of the Logos Himself, the *first-begotten*.

Therefore, there would seem little doubt that Justin says that Consecration was effected by Prayer for the Logos—the Second Person of the Trinity.

And such an Invocation we find in Bishop Serapion's Prayer Book.

We therefore gather this idea of the Office which he describes:

> Lections
> Sermons
> Congregational Intercession
> Kiss
> Offertory
> (Extemporary) {Prayers
> {Thanksgivings
> A Consecration by Invocation of the Logos
> The Administration

IV. *S. Cyril's Account.*

He was lecturing in the fourth century to the Catechumens at Jerusalem on the Mass of the Faithful. The earlier part of the Service (the Mass of the Catechumens) was familiar to them from their attendance at it.

His account (Brightman, *Liturgies Eastern and Western*, Appendix B) begins (after the bread and wine are on the altar) with the *Lavabo.* "Then cries the Deacon, 'Take one another and let us *Kiss* each other.'

"After this the Priest cries, '*Lift up your hearts* (Ἄνω τὰς καρδίας).'

"Then ye respond, '*We lift them up unto the Lord*' (lit. we have them towards the Lord, ἔχομεν πρὸς Κύριον).

"After this the Priest says, '*Let us give thanks* (εὐχαριστῶμεν) to the Lord.'

"And then ye say, '*It is meet and right* (ἄξιον καὶ δίκαιον).'

"After this we make mention of *heaven and earth* and sea, sun, moon, and stars and all creatures reasoning and unreasoning, visible and invisible; *Archangels*, Powers, Dominions, Principalities, Virtues, Thrones, many-faced *cherubim* and *seraphim* which...say, *Holy*, *Holy*, *Holy*, Lord of Hosts....

"This we recite that we may be sharers in the hymn with the heavenly host.

"Then[1] after sanctifying ourselves with these spiritual hymns we *beseech* the kind GOD to *send down* (ἐξαποστεῖλαι) *the Holy Spirit upon the gifts* (ἐπὶ τὰ προκείμενα) that He may make the bread the BODY of Christ and the wine the BLOOD of Christ.

"And then after the completion of the spiritual sacrifice, the unbloody worship, over that sacrifice (ἐπὶ τῆς θυσίας ἐκείνης) of the propitiation (τοῦ ἱλασμοῦ) we *beseech* GOD for the common peace of the Churches, for the good order of the World, for Kings, for Generals... for those in sickness, for the distressed and in (general) one word (ἁπαξαπλῶς) for all who need help we all intercede and offer this sacrifice (ταύτην προσφέρομεν τὴν θυσίαν). And then we make mention of all who have fallen asleep before us....

"And then after this we say that Prayer which the Saviour gave to His own disciples...Our Father...evil.

---

[1] S. Cyril makes no mention of the recitation of the narrative of Institution but he had already lectured on it.

And then after the finish of the Prayer you will say ' Amen.'

"After this the Priest says, ' The Holy things to the Holy.' Then ye say, ' There is One Holy, One Lord Jesus Christ.'

"After this ye hear the *Communion Psalms* (lxiii. and xxxv.). Meanwhile approaching to the Holy Altar of GOD...*receive*....

"And awaiting the prayer, *give thanks* to GOD who counted thee worthy of so great mysteries."

In this we notice the Lavabo, the Kiss, the Eucharistic Act (Sursum Corda and bidding of Praise and their Responds, the Preface (as we call it) and the Sanctus), the Invocation of the Spirit, the Intercession for Living and Departed, Lord's Prayer, Elevation, Communion and a final prayer of Thanksgiving or Blessing.

Comparing this with the narrative of Justin, we see one startling change[1], the transference of the Intercession from the Offertory to the central part of the Office—the Consecration and Invocation.

And we see the Invocation, which in Irenaeus was spoken of only as an " Invocation of GOD," and in Justin as an Invocation of the Logos, converted into an Invocation of the Spirit.

[1] Although the Didache seems to have the Intercession after Consecration.

CHAPTER III

THE EASTERN LITURGIES

THE 4th century is judged to be the date of a whole crop of pseudo-primitive "Church Orders." These were collections of Canons and regulations for discipline and worship which contained references in varying degrees of fulness to the Eucharistic Office. The chief documents are the Canons of Hippolytus, the Ethiopian Church Order, the Testament of Our Lord and the Apostolic Constitutions.

The accounts of the Office in these manifest a substantial agreement. The fullest and the most famous is that in the VIIIth book of the Apostolic Constitutions which commonly bears the name of the "Clementine Liturgy." It purports to be a complete Liturgy composed by S. Clement, Bishop of Rome, at the end of the 1st century. The claim is incapable of substantiation. And the whole work of the Apostolic Constitutions is believed, as a result of the latest investigation, to be the work of the Pseudo-Ignatius and composed at Antioch in the second half of the 4th century.

In fact this Liturgy represents the Syrian family of the Eastern type of Liturgies.

The principal real example of the Syrian Liturgy is the Greek Liturgy of S. James.

The earliest mention of this is in the 32nd Canon of the Council of Trullo in 692, where it is cited as the authentic work of S. James the Lord's brother. But the close identity with it of the Syriac Liturgy of S. James used by the Jacobites proves its great antiquity. For it must have attained the sanction of long use and authority before the separation of that body from Catholic Communion in the 6th century.

We will take the "Clementine" for description, pointing out where S. James differs.

The Clementine form (Brightman, *Liturgies Eastern and Western*, Vol. I. pp. 3 and sq.) begins with the Reading of the Lections (the Law of the Prophets and of our Epistles and of the Acts and of the Gospels).

[S. James (Brightman, *op. cit.* pp. 31 and sq.) opens with Preparation, Hymn Trisagion, Lections from Old Testament, Prophets, Epistle and Gospel, interspersed with Antiphons and prayers.]

Then the Salutation, Sermon and Dismissals of Catechumens, Penitents, etc. with prayers.

[S. James has no Dismissals.]

The *Mass of the Faithful* begins with the Synapte or Litany said by the Deacon, the varied petitions of which are summed up in a solemn prayer by the Bishop.

[S. James has here the "Great Entrance" with the "Gifts," preceded by the Prayer of the Incense and accompanied by prayer; the Creed.]

Next came a Blessing, Kiss and Salutation, Lavabo.

[S. James has "An Inclination or prayer of humble approach."]

The Offertory (without provided prayers, but with prayer in S. James).

Then the Anaphora:

1. The *Eucharistic Act*, consisting of Sursum Corda and Invitation to "give thanks," followed by their Responds, the Preface (as we should call it) of great length, and the Ter Sanctus.

2. The *Consecration Section*.

In this is commemorated the Mercy of Redemption, the Incarnation, Passion, Death, and Resurrection, the Command, and the Narrative of Institution.

3 and 4. The Prayer of *Oblation and Invocation* follow.

"Therefore, having in remembrance His Passion and death and resurrection and His return into heaven and His future second Advent...we offer unto Thee...this bread and this cup...And we implore Thee to look graciously upon these gifts...and to send down upon this Sacrifice Thy Holy Spirit...that He may declare[1] this bread the Body of Thy Christ and this cup the Blood of Thy Christ...."

5. Next the *Great Intercession*...for the whole Church, celebrant, King, all who from the beginning have pleased Thee (i.e. faithful departed), congregation present, city, sick, slaves, exiles, travellers, persecutors, catechumens, penitents, for the fruits of the earth, for the absent and for all—concluding with a Doxology, to which the people say "Amen."

[In S. James the Diptychs or lists of the living to

---

[1] ἀποφήνῃ, S. James "hallow and make" (ἁγιάσῃ καὶ ποιῇ).

be prayed for were read in the course of this, and definite Intercession made at length for the Departed.]

6. And the *Lord's Prayer* with proëm and embolismus followed.

7. After this the *Inclination* or short Litany with prayer for worthy Reception.

8. Then the *Elevation* and the Proclamation " Holy things for holy people."

[S. James adds—Fraction and Consignation and Commixture of the Elements.]

9. The Communion.

10. The Thanksgiving for Communion.

11. Prayer for the people (S. James, " an Inclination ").

12. The Dismissal.

This is the general Eastern type. To it the Byzantine Rite (represented by the Liturgies of S. Basil, S. Chrysostom, and Armenia) closely conforms.

The chief variations from this arrangement are :

(1) The Intercession is placed after the Narrative of Institution and before the solemn Oblation in the Assyrian and Nestorian Liturgies.

(2) The Intercession is placed in the midst of the Eucharistic Act (the " Preface ") in the later forms of the Alexandrine Rite presented in the Greek S. Mark (of probably the 5th century), the Coptic and Abyssinian. [But the most ancient member of this family, Bishop Serapion's Prayer Book, follows the general norm in this matter.]

CHAPTER IV

THE WESTERN LITURGIES

In the West up to the beginning of the 5th century, there were two types of Office in use—the " Gallican," as it is generally called, and the Roman.

The Gallican was in use in North Italy, Gaul, Spain, Britain and Ireland. The Roman was in use at Rome, in South Italy and in Africa.

I. *The Gallican Rite.*

The Gallican shows considerable affinities with the Eastern Liturgies, and not only in structure, for some of its forms agree verbatim with those of the Syro-Byzantine forms of the 4th century.

This character has generally been assumed to be due to the Eastern origin of the Church of Lyons. Duchesne (*Christian Worship*, S.P.C.K. pp. 90 sq.) however attributes it to the Episcopate of Auxentius, a Cappadocian, at Milan in the 4th century—then the commanding city of the West.

In describing this Rite we may take the account of the Office in use at Paris in the 6th century given by S. Germain, with notes of the variations in the Mozarabic Rite in use in Spain and in the Ambrosian

Rite of Milan which was early modified in a Roman direction. (Duchesne, *Christian Worship*, S.P.C.K. pp. 189 and sqq.)

The Introit.

Introductory Canticles. Trisagion, Kyrie and Benedictus called "Prophetia."

The Mozarabic and Ambrosian have the "Gloria in Excelsis" in place of "Trisagion": and the Mozarabic has no Kyrie.

Collectio post "prophetiam."

In the Ambrosian an "Oratio" precedes the "Gloria."

Lections.

Homily.

The Mass of the Faithful.

Litany (of the Oriental type) and Collectio post precem ("Levitæ pro populo deprecentur et sacerdotes... pro peccato populi intercedent...." S. Germain).

This is absent from the Mozarabic and Ambrosian, though on Sundays in Lent there is a Litany in the Mozarabic before the Epistle and in the Ambrosian after the Ingressa or "Introit."

Dismissals of Catechumens, etc. (absent in the Mozarabic and Ambrosian).

Offertory. Procession of the Oblation with Canticles.

Here the Mozarabic and Ambrosian introduce a prayer corresponding to the Prayer of the Veil in Eastern Liturgies—preceded by an exhortation called "Praefatio Missae."

The Intercession. The Diptychs of Departed and "Collectio post nomina."

The Ambrosian omits these and the Kiss that follows, from this place following the Roman arrangement and form.

The *Kiss* and *Collect*. The Mozarabic puts the Collect before the Kiss.

The Eucharistic Act. Sursum Corda, etc.

" Preface " called " Contestatio " or " Immolatio " in Gaul and " Illatio " in Spain.

Sanctus.

Collectio post Sanctus—which is not in the Ambrosian Rite except in the Mass for the Saturday in Holy Week.

This after the Eastern manner is a thanksgiving for the Mercy of the Incarnation and Redemption leading up to the Narrative of Institution.

The Consecration. The last sentence of the Narrative of Institution is identical in all three and the Clementine and S. James and other Eastern Liturgies.

Oblation and Invocation—a prayer called " post secreta, post pridie, post mysterium ": e.g. " Haec... oramus uti hoc sacrificium suscipere et sanctificare digneris : ut fiat nobis Eucharistia legitima...in transformationem corporis ac sanguinis," etc.

The Elevation.

The Fraction—during which the " Confractorium " was sung—but in the Mozarabic " *the Creed.*"

The Lord's Prayer.

The Commixture. In the Ambrosian as in the Roman, the Commixture is joined to the Fraction before the Lord's Prayer.

Benediction.   The Ambrosian places the Kiss here.
Communion.
Thanksgiving.
Dismissal.

II. *The Roman Rite.*

Of this there is no really ancient transcription. We
have various editions, bearing the names of Leonine,
Gelasian and Gregorian.   But internal evidence shows
a later date in each case than the name which they
bear would suggest.   They probably represent the uses
of the late 6th, 7th and 8th centuries.

The Canon in the main probably has been unaltered
since the 4th century : except that Pope Gregory added
the paragraph " diesque, etc." to " Hanc Igitur " and
transferred the Lord's Prayer from after the Manual
Acts to the end of the Canon after the Greek model :
and S. Leo added " sanctum...hostiam " to " Supra
quae," on the testimony of the author of *Liber Pontifi-*
calis c. beginning of 6th century.

The Roman Rite naturally was brought to England
by S. Augustine, with the liberty granted to him by
the Pope of introducing modification from the Gallican
use prevailing.

The Revision of S. Osmund of the Sarum Missal,
in the 11th century, was to bring it into close and
practical identity with the Roman Mass in general
detail and specially in the structure and Canon.

The order is as follows :

The Kyrie.

Gloria in Excelsis—a Greek morning hymn, originated here by its use at the first Mass of the Nativity at daybreak.

Collecta.

Lections.

The Creed [introduced in the 11th century].

"*Oremus*," remnant of the *Intercession*. There is no prayer here except on Good Friday[1]. In the 8th century, prayers here are found on Wednesday as well as Friday in Holy Week. Their tenor is not specially connected with the Passion, but for ordinary needs, such as are common in Eastern Liturgies.

The Offertory and Collecta super Oblata. These correspond to the Collects in the Eastern prothesis. The early Sacramentaries had *no* prayers. During the Offertory was sung the "Offertorium," now attenuated to a single verse.

The Eucharistic Act. Sursum, etc.

Preface.

Sanctus.

Part of the Intercession. A long passage enumerating the persons in whose name the Oblation is made, viz. Te igitur ... Memento ... Communicantes ... Hanc igitur.... These correspond to the Recitation of the Diptychs which in the Gallican and Eastern Liturgies preceded the Eucharistic Prayer.

An *Invocation* (quam Oblationem — see later, Chapter VIII.).

The Narrative of Institution.

N.B. There is absent the feature found in Eastern

---

[1] And in Requiems.

and Gallican usage, viz. a thanksgiving for the Incarnation and Redemption, to connect the general Praise and Thanksgiving of the Sanctus and the Narrative of Institution.

Oblation $\begin{cases} \text{Unde et memores.} \\ \text{Supra quae.} \\ \text{Supplices te.} \end{cases}$

The Intercession (remainder).   Memento—for departed, but " Nobisque " brings in the living. And so it corresponds to the Eastern position of the Intercession[1].

The Lord's Prayer, placed here by S. Gregory after the Eastern model.

The Fraction and Commixture.

The Kiss.

Preparation of Communicants.   Two Collects since 8th century.   Prior to S. Gregory the Lord's Prayer was so used here.

The Communion.

Post-Communion or Thanksgiving and Dismissal.

In comparing these two types of Office used in the West, the principal difference to be noted is the treatment of the Intercession.

In the Gallican type it is in connection with the Offertory.

In the Roman it is divided and placed, part before the Commemoration of Christ's work and Institution, and part after the form corresponding to the Oblation in the Eastern Liturgies.

---

[1] " Per quem...semper bona creas " is probably due to a prayer, originally preceding this, for the fruits of the earth to be given.

NOTE ON CHAPTERS III AND IV

COMPARATIVE TABLE OF EASTERN AND WESTERN STRUCTURES

Main features of General Eastern Type	Main features of Gallican Type	Main features of Roman Type
(1) Litany	(1) Litany[1]	(1) "Oremus"
(2) Offertory	(2) Offertory	(2) Offertory
[Intercession: in Justin]	(8) The Intercession	——
(3) Eucharistic Act	(3) Eucharistic Act	(3) Eucharistic Act
——	——	(8) Part of Intercession
(4) Commemoration of Redemption	(4) Commemoration of Redemption	(7) Invocation
(5) and Narrative of Institution	(5) and Narrative of Institution	(5) Narrative of Institution
(6) Prayer of Oblation	(6) Prayer of Oblation	(6) Prayer of Oblation
(7) and Invocation	(7) and Invocation	
(8) The Intercession	——	(8) and Rest of Intercession
——	(10) The Elevation and Fraction	——
(9) Communicants' Preparation: Lord's Prayer and Inclination	(9) Communicants' Preparation: Lord's Prayer[2] and Benediction	(9) Communicants' Preparation: Lord's Prayer
(10) Elevation and Manual Acts	——	(10) Manual Acts
		(9) Preparation of Communicants: 2 Collects
(11) The Communion	(11) The Communion	(11) The Communion
(12) The Thanksgiving	(12) The Thanksgiving	(12) Thanksgiving
(13) Prayer and Dismissal	(13) The Dismissal	(13) Dismissal

[1] In *Mozarabic* the Litany is absent.

[2] The Commixture came between the Lord's Prayer and Blessing in *Mozarabic*.

CHAPTER V

THE FIRST PRAYER BOOK OF EDWARD VI

BEFORE coming to the review of our present Office, it will be advisable to consider the First Prayer Book of Edward VI, which was the first Prayer Book in the English tongue. There had been an "Order of Communion" in the previous year 1548—but this was merely the provision for the intercalation of the Form for the preparation of Communicants into the old Office.

The Office of 1549 was purely a revision of the Sarum Office modified by some acquaintance with the Eastern (and it may be Mozarabic) Rites and Lutheran Services.

The Liturgies of S. Chrysostom and S. Basil were printed and known to English leaders. For example, Fisher had a Latin translation of the Liturgy of S. Chrysostom[1] given him by Erasmus in 1510-1 and also had copies of S. Basil[2] and S. Chrysostom lent him by Bishop Stokesley of London in 1526. Cranmer[3] too is known to have studied S. Chrysostom.

---

[1] Fisher, *De Veritate Corporis* f. 64 a : and the copy is in the Cambridge University Library.

[2] *Ib*. 64 a, 87 a.

[3] His copy in Erasmus' Latin Version with his autograph is in the British Museum.

The new form began with

The Lord's Prayer and Collect for Purity (" Almighty GOD to Whom all hearts," etc.);

The Introit;

Lesser Litany; and the

Gloria in Excelsis.

Then came—Prayer for the Sovereign (see note);

The Collect and Lections (omitting the Canticles by old and general custom connected with them);

The Creed;

Homily and Exhortation (" Dearly beloved in the Lord," etc.).

It omitted the " Oremus" of the Latin Rite before the Offertory and the prayers with which the Elements were offered.

After the Offertory came the *Great Eucharistic Act*.

Then it brought together the *Intercession* (divided in the Sarum Rite) and placed it here before the Consecration.

The Consecration, like the Latin Rite (of which the Office was a Revision), lacked the Thanksgiving for the Incarnation and Redemption with which the Eastern and Gallican led up from the Sanctus to the Narrative of the Institution.

But there was a new feature—a form of prayer was *prefaced to the Narrative of Institution*, consisting of two parts:

(i) a recital of the mercy of GOD in giving His Son to be the Unique Sacrifice; and of the fact of His Ordinance of this " Perpetual memory of It":

(ii) an *Invocation* of the Holy Spirit and "Word" on the Elements.

The words of Institution were in the very terms of S. Paul, and after the Mozarabic and Greek models.

After the Narrative of Institution followed the *Great Oblation* and the Lord's Prayer; omitting the Embolismus to the Lord's Prayer and the Fraction and Commixture and Kiss with their devotions after the same Prayer. But it contained a Salutation of Peace, and after that introduced a new feature, issued the previous year for use in the course of the old Office, viz. the *Communicants' Preparation*. This consisted of Invitation ("Ye that do truly repent," etc.), Confession, Absolution, "Comfortable" Words and Prayer of Humble Access ("We do not presume," etc.)—all of which are familiar in our present Office.

Then came the *Communion*—accompanied by the Agnus Dei and followed by various sentences of Scripture, called the Post-Communion; the *Thanksgiving* ("Almighty and everliving GOD," etc.) and the *Blessing* ("the peace of GOD," etc.) in place of the Deacon's Dismissal "Ite missa est."

NOTE. The prayer for the Sovereign was introduced into the beginning of the Office in order that when the Service closed with the Offertory, concluding Collects and Blessing, without the complete Office being celebrated, there might be a prayer for the Sovereign.

CHAPTER VI

OUR PRESENT OFFICE

IT opens like the Office of 1549 with the *Lord's Prayer and Collect* for Purity. Then in place of the Gloria in Excelsis or other hymn of praise, universally found in the beginning of the Office, we have the *Ten Commandments*, each followed by the Kyrie. The idea probably was to provide a substitute for the obligatory system of Private Confession, by thus moving to self-examination and stirring to repentance at the threshold of the Service. Yet it may be questioned whether this feature does not strike a note in the Service of Praise and Thanksgiving alien to the character of the Service and to the " boldness[1] " with which the children should approach the Throne of Grace.

Then the Prayer for the Sovereign ;

The *Collect and Lections and Creed* as in the Office of 1549 ;

Then the Homily.

Then we come to the *Offertory*—sentences of Scripture after the old precedent, said or sung during the

---

[1] Cp. Hebrews x. 22.

collection of the people's alms and preceding the Lesser
Oblation of the Elements. For the actual placing of
the Elements on the Altar, as in 1549, no prayer or word
is provided.

After this we have the Prayer for the Church
Militant, which is the *Great Intercession*—placed in
connection *with the Offertory, instead of with the Consecration.*

From this General Intercession we miss the commemoration of the Saints by name and any explicit
intercession for the departed.

Then we have the Exhortation placed after the
Sermon in 1549 and part of the *Preparation of Communicants,* viz. the Invitation, Confession, Absolution,
and Comfortable Words.

Next·is placed the *Great Eucharistic Act* (Sursum
Corda, etc., Preface and Ter Sanctus).

The Prayer of Humble Access succeeds a prayer for
worthy reception and of self-humiliation.

The *Prayer of Consecration* follows in the form of
1549, with the same Collect-like introduction in place
of the ancient phrasing of praise for the Incarnation
and Redemption: but the explicit *Invocation* of the
Holy Spirit and Word is omitted.

The Office goes on at once to the *Communion.*

After this is placed the *Lord's Prayer,* as an act of
praise, with the Doxology, instead of occurring in its
universal place before Communion as an Act of
Preparation.

Then *two prayers* for interchangeable use—the

former is the form of *Oblation* joined in 1549 to the Prayer of Consecration; the latter the *Thanksgiving* after Communion of 1549.

The *Gloria in Excelsis* then follows as a final Act of Thanksgiving, Pleading and Adoration—the one good feature of the changes made in 1552.

The *Blessing* concludes the Office.

In reviewing the whole we note the separation of (1) the Great Intercession and of (2) the Prayer of Oblation from the Commemoration of the Institution, leaving the Solemn Act of Consecration without the form of offering the Memorial in words or of pleading It in intercession.

(3) We see also the separation of the Eucharistic Act from the Commemoration of the Institution, and the absence of the primitive thanksgiving for Redemption before the Narrative of Institution.

For the first of these features primitive precedent may be alleged. The others are unique.

(4) There is also an absence of explicit Invocation of the Divine Power to fit the Elements for their sacred use.

(5) There is no form for the verbal Oblation of the Elements.

(6) The Great Intercession is defective in its reference to the departed.

The absence of the Lord's Prayer from the end of the Canon is unparalleled, except in the account given by Justin and in the " Clementine " Liturgy. And the division of the Communicants' Preparation and its place before the Consecration, instead of immediately before Communion, is not after the usual manner.

These are points which may be termed the defects of our present English Communion Office, though not perhaps defects of equal gravity. It will be our object to endeavour to take these in turn into more detailed consideration.

While we may notice the absence of provision for the Manual Acts (Consignation or Commixture) or Elevation—all but universal.

CHAPTER VII

THE SEPARATION OF THE INTERCESSION
FROM THE CONSECRATION

As the Service was instituted to be a "perpetual
memory" of Christ's "precious death," it naturally is
the occasion for intercession. If we plead the Sacrifice,
it is natural to have, and to mention, special objects
for which the pleading is made. So there has always
been in the Office a Solemn Intercession.

And as the Intercession is a specification of the
objects for which the Memorial is offered, the logical
and natural place for its occurrence would seem to be
after Commemoration has been made before GOD of
His Work of Redemption, and of the Institution as the
ground for what is being done, and after His acceptance
of our Offering has been asked.

Thus the Intercession would come after the solemn
Oblation.

And this is the position in the description of the
Eucharistic Service given by S. Cyril of Jerusalem in
347 and in the "Clementine" Liturgy[1]. And this is
the general position in the Eastern Liturgies, except in
the Alexandrine family and the Nestorian Rite. In the
former it occurs in the course of the Eucharistic Act
before the Commemoration, and in the latter immedi-

[1] And also perhaps in the Didache.

ately after the Commemoration of the Institution and before the Prayer of Oblation. (Brightman, *Liturgies Eastern and Western*, Vol. I. *in loc.*)

In the Latin Rite it is split in two parts, one preceding the Commemoration of Institution, the other following; the former consisting of petitions for the Church, for rulers in Church and State and for the living, together with commemoration of the Saints; the latter consisting of prayers for the departed and for the congregation.

The First Prayer Book of Edward VI brought all this Intercession together, before the Commemoration of Redemption and Institution.

In our Prayer Book, the Intercession comes, entirely cut off from the main central part of the Office, immediately after the Offertory. This change was made in 1552 and is generally supposed to have been due to the desire to so rearrange the Office as to obscure the Memorial and make the Communion the centre.

This was probably the great desire and aim of the advanced reformers.

But I venture to think that Cranmer's change is not solely due to wanton desire for drastic revolution, but to his deference to Justin Martyr. He refers to Justin and Irenaeus in his writings[1] constantly as " authors nearest to Christ's time and therefore knowing best the truth." He made a great point of Justin's

---

[1] e.g. in his " Defence of the true Doctrine of the Eucharist " and his " Answer to the Crafty Cavillation of Gardiner " (Parker Society), p. 263.

making no mention of any Invocation (*vide* Chapter VIII. on "Absence of Explicit Invocation") and based his support of the sufficiency of the words of Institution alone, for Consecration, on Justin.

All this would seem to indicate a settled conviction, that Justin is the oldest witness, therefore the truest, and therefore to be followed entirely before all others.

Now Justin (*Apol.* I. c. LXV. § 1) says that before the Offertory the Congregation utter united (κοινὰς) prayers for all and (*Apol.* I. c. LXVII. § 5) that after the Offertory "the President sent up prayers." And this connection with the Offertory was maintained in the Gallican use both at Paris in the 6th century, according to S. Germain's account, and in the Mozarabic Rite of Spain; while the "Oremus," without any intercessions except on Good Friday[1], in the Latin Rite before the Offertory is a testimony to the original position there of the Intercession in the earliest Roman Office.

The present Roman Office is palpably a compromise. The former portion of the Intercession is the original Intercession pushed forward from the Offertory. The latter portion is an addition to assimilate the use to the Eastern structure.

Moreover in the Eastern Liturgies[2] there is a Litany and Collect at the opening of the Mass of the Faithful, before the Offertory, though in the Byzantine

---

[1] In Requiems also there is a prayer here—an Offertory prayer with Intercession for the Departed.

[2] e.g. Brightman, *Liturgies Eastern and Western*, Vol. I. pp. 9–12, 38–9, 120–2.

family[1] the growth of the ceremonies of the Great Entrance has pushed this Litany back into the Mass of the Catechumens, after the Lections.

Therefore, after the testimony of Justin and the example of the Gallican Rite, we may conclude that the place of our Intercession has good and primitive precedent. And this precedent finds further strength in the evidence furnished by the "Oremus" in the Latin Rite and the earlier Litany in the Eastern Rites.

This was evidently the conclusion of Seabury and of the compilers and revisers of the American Prayer Book in 1790, when they permitted its continuance in the English position.

At the same time, defensible and of ancient precedent as it is, this position appears to me a *defect* in our Office.

1. *On historical grounds.* In the earliest days ideas were like to be crude and ill-formed[2]. Passing

---

[1] *Ibid.* 262 sq., 310 sq.

[2] It may well be, that the first age did not fully distinguish between the Oblation of the Elements in themselves for the use of God's Service and the Mystical Oblation of Christ made when the Priest takes them and reproduces in word and action what Christ did at the Institution.

[This would be parallel to the early want of distinction between the work of Christ and the Holy Spirit, which for example made Justin (*Ap.* I. xxxiii.) ascribe the Incarnation to the power of the Logos —though the Church early made it an article of belief, that it was through the Holy Ghost.]

Accordingly there was only one time of Oblation in mind, the Offertory, and therefore with this the Intercessions were connected.

Later, minds cleared, and the two offerings became distinguished. The Alexandrine family would seem to occupy a transitional position.

years brought deeper insight into the purpose and meaning of the Eucharist. The Holy Spirit's guidance was not limited to the very first age alone. And very early we find the later position after the Commemoration of Institution and the Oblation. This was the position[1] in S. Cyril's account of 347. This was the position in which it is found in the Prayer Book of Bishop Serapion of the middle of the same century. The inference from this identity of use in Egypt and Jerusalem is, surely, the very ancient date of this arrangement, probably well within a century of Justin's account.

The same position was that adopted by general consent of the East, and maintained all along the years since then.

The conclusion would seem to be, that though the connection of the Intercession with the Offertory is the most primitive, yet the connection with the Great Oblation following the Commemoration of the Institution is of not much less antiquity and of wider adoption.

2. *On logical grounds.* The Intercession obviously

Bishop Serapion (ed. Wordsworth, S.P.C.K. p. 62) just before the Narrative of Institution says, "To Thee we *have* offered this bread, the likeness of the Body of the only begotten. This bread is the likeness...because the Lord Jesus Christ in the night, etc....Wherefore we...have offered...": and similarly with regard to the cup. S. Mark also at the time of Oblation and Narrative of Institution, speaks of the Offering in the past tense instead of the present (προεθήκαμεν instead of προσφέρομεν of the Clementine, S. James, Byzantine, etc.). (Brightman, *Liturgies Eastern and Western*, Vol. I. p. 133, l. 30.)

[1] And possibly in the Order given in the Didache.

depends on the pleading of Christ's work. Surely it should follow the pleading on which it depends and not precede, separated by various other ideas and actions. It is usual first to present credentials, and then state demands: first to state the ground for a request before making it.

So the preface to the Nonjurors' Liturgy of 1718 says, "The prayer for the Whole State of Christ's Church...after the prayer for Consecration. For when the Sacrifice, commemorative of that upon the Cross, is finished, and God the Father propitiated by this Memorial; it is then the most proper time to declare the ends of the Oblation, and recommend the Church to Divine Protection."

3. *On practical grounds.* The generality of people are neither instructed in Liturgiology, nor are they in the habit of reflecting on the rationale of things. Consequently they fail to realise the connection between the Intercession and the pleading of Christ's Sacrifice in the Consecration. Ultimately the position is one of indifference, because the Office is one Whole. But practically it is of the utmost importance. The arrangement of the Office ought to convey easily and naturally its main ideas to the unlearned. And in fact, I venture to say, it is a matter of difficulty for the well informed and devout to keep the connection in mind. Hence it is, that general custom inserts in manuals of devotion, intercessions for use after the Consecration, because the defect and want in our Office is felt, and because it is asking too much of human nature to think

of the Consecration and Oblation while the Prayer for the Church Militant is being said, and to base this latter on the former.

And this difficulty of connection has largely been transformed into a distinct severance in thought. The unhappy customs of ending the Service after the Prayer for the Church, or of making a pause there, or of going out of Church at that point, have all tended to separate the Intercession entirely from the Consecration in the minds of the people. The majority, so far from seeing the connection, would say that there is no connection.

Hence, while the position of the Intercession in our Office is after primitive example and as sufficient to obtain its answer there as after the Consecration, and affords no reason for interpolating the Intercessions of the Latin Rite into our Office, yet I venture to think it is a defect in our Office. And on practical grounds it is a hindrance and a stumblingblock to the people at large. If only our Office commemorated and pleaded Christ's work, and then urged our petitions on the ground of that pleading, it would give a greater reality to the Intercession, and greater comfort and assurance to the worshippers[1].

[1] In this the Scottish Rite of 1764 and Bishop Seabury's Office of 1786 show us the way. The prayer for the Church follows the Oblation prayer joined to the Consecration prayer.

CHAPTER VIII

ABSENCE OF EXPLICIT INVOCATION

As we remarked at the outset, the fitness of things would seem to require some petition that GOD would fit the natural elements for the sacred purpose which they are to serve.

This feeling found expression from the first in some form. And from the first half of the 4th century it showed itself in a prayer for the Illapse of the Holy Spirit. S. Cyril in his Lectures (A.D. 347) says: "after sanctifying ourselves with these spiritual hymns (the Sanctus, etc.) we beseech the kind GOD to send down the Holy Spirit upon the Gifts, that He may make the Bread the BODY of Christ and the Wine the BLOOD of Christ[1]."

This form of Invocation is universal in the Eastern Liturgies (except Bishop Serapion), and this is the substance of the general form.

There are variations: e.g.

(1) The Prayer Book of Bishop Serapion (ed. Wordsworth (S.P.C.K.) p. 63) calls for the descent of the "Holy Word" instead of the Holy Spirit.

This is in accordance too with the statement of

[1] Brightman, *Liturgies Eastern and Western*, Vol. I. p. 465.

Justin (*Ap.* I. LXVI.).   And there are other instances of the same.

In a fragment of a "Sermon to the Baptised" quoted as the words of S. Athanasius by Eutychius in the 6th century in his sermon "On the Pasch and most Holy Eucharist," we find testimony to a similar use.   "When the great prayers and the holy supplications are sent up to GOD, the WORD descends upon the bread and the cup and they become His BODY" (*P. G.* XXVI. 1325).

And in the Gothic Missal in the Advent Mass, the Post Secreta in the place of the Invocation prays "Descendat ... super haec, quae tibi offerimus, *Verbum tuum sanctum*; descendat...spiritus; descendat antiquae indulgentiae tuae donum, ut fiat Oblatio," etc. Mabillon, *De Lit. Gall.* p. 335.

(2)   Instead of asking that the Holy Ghost may "*make the Bread the Body of Christ*," etc.

(*a*)   the "Clementine[1]" has ἀποφήνη and S. Basil's[2] Liturgy has ἀναδεῖξαι ("show the bread to be the BODY," etc.).

(*β*)   Bishop Serapion's[3] form is "that the bread may become the BODY," etc.

(*γ*)   The Nestorian[4] and Malabar[5] Rites have "let Him rest on this offering...that it may be to us for the pardon," etc.—referring only to the effects or "virtus

[1] Brightman, *Liturgies Eastern and Western*, Vol. I. p. 21.
[2] *Ibid.* p. 329.   [3] Ed. Wordsworth, S.P.C.K. p. 63.
[4] Brightman, *op. cit.* p. 387.
[5] Neale and Littledale, *Liturgies*, Trans., ed. 2, p. 167.

sacramenti," and not to the " res sacramenti " or " inward part."

(δ)   Like S. Cyril's[1] account, the Clementine, Bishop Serapion, S. Mark[2], the Abyssinian[3], Jacobite, the Nestorian and Malabar Rites make the object of the Divine action the offering only. The other[4] rites add the worshippers as an object: " Send down...*upon us* and on these gifts."   All place the Invocation after the Narrative of Institution and in the course of the Prayer of Oblation.

Praise was offered for the blessings of creation and as the due of creatures, and for Redemption by the Redeemed.   Then the Institution of this Memorial by the Redeemer is narrated and solemnly imitated.

Acceptance of these gifts, which He appointed, is asked and then prayer is made for the intervention of the Holy Spirit to make them the Body and Blood of Christ.

For example, the Clementine[5], after the Narrative of Institution, has "Therefore...we offer unto Thee... this bread and this cup...and we implore Thee to... send down upon this Sacrifice Thy Holy Spirit...that He may declare (the other Liturgies "make") this bread the BODY of thy Christ," etc.

In the West, the *Gallican Rite* had an invocation originally, as was to be expected from its Eastern origin.

[1] Brightman, *op. cit.* p. 465.
[2] *Ibid.* p. 134.   [3] *Ibid.* p. 233.
[4] e.g. S. James, Brightman, *op. cit.* p. 53, Byzantine Rites, p. 329.
[5] Brightman, *op. cit.* p. 20 sq.

Isidore writes: " porro sexta (oratio) ex hinc succedit, conformatio Sacramenti, ut oblatio quae Deo offertur, sanctificata per spiritum sanctum, Christi corpori ac sanguini conformetur " (Mabillon, *De Lit. Gall.* p. 10).

In the Gothic Mass, however, for the Vigil of Easter (Mabillon XXXVI.) the Invocation comes in the " Post Sanctus " before the Narrative of Institution : " we pray that Thou wilt bless this sacrifice with Thy blessing and pour upon it the dew of thy Holy Spirit, that it may be a valid (legitima) Eucharist to all who receive it."

But this is unusual.   Ordinarily it occupies the Eastern position after the Narrative of Institution.

In the Gothic Mass for the Assumption : " Let there descend, O Lord, on these Sacrifices of Thy blessing, the coeternal and co-working Paraclete, the Spirit, that...the bread translated into the BODY and the cup into the BLOOD, it may avail," etc. (Mabillon XII.).

But the definite Invocation soon began to disappear.

Thus—" let there descend here Thy blessing on this bread and cup in the transformation of Thy Holy Spirit " (Mabillon LXV.).

Two offices of the Missale Gallicanum Vetus (Mabillon I. and V.) have a triple Invocation of the vaguer sort : " Let there descend, we pray, Almighty GOD, on these things which we offer Thee, Thy Holy Word ; Let there descend the Spirit of Thy inestimable Glory, let there descend the gift of Thy ancient favour (indulgentiae), that our oblation may become a spiritual host accepted for a savour of sweetness," etc.

And in the Mozarabic Missal, in the Office for the Nativity[1], we have this prayer after the Narrative:

"Haec, Domine, dona tua et praecepta servantes, in altare tuum Panis et Vini holocausta proponimus, rogantes profundissimam tuae misericordiae pietatem, ut in eodem spiritu, quo Te in carne Virginitas incorrupta concepit, has hostias Trinitas indivisa sanctificet," etc.

The *Roman Rite* had no direct Invocation in any known MSS., but testimony to the presence originally of an Invocation is found in Optatus of Milevis c. 368 (in *De Schism. Don.* vi., *P.L.* XI. 1065); he speaks of the altars as places "where GOD Almighty is invoked; where the Holy Spirit descends at the Church's prayer."

This very early disappeared. But though there is no direct Invocation of the Holy Spirit there is a prayer (Quam oblationem) *before* the Narrative of Institution, in which GOD is asked to bless the Oblation that "it may become to us the BODY and BLOOD," etc.

There is, indeed, also, in the place occupied in the Oriental norm by the Invocation, a prayer often interpreted as such. "Supplices Te rogamus, omnipotens Deus, jube haec perferri per manus sancti angeli tui in sublime altare tuum in conspectu Divinae Majestatis tuae, ut quotquot ex hac altaris participatione sacrosanctum Filii tui corpus et sanguinem sumpserimus, omni benedictione coelesti et gratia repleamur." But such an interpretation is forced, and unsupported by the ancient commentators. There is in it no prayer

[1] *P.L.*, Migne, tom. LXXXV. i. 189.

for the coming down of Divine power, but for the acceptance of the Offering on high, or perhaps rather, of the prayers[1], only (as many interpreters think), and the end in view is not any change in the Elements[1], but the receiving of Divine grace by the communicants.

With regard to the other prayer before the Narrative of Institution the case is different. By its plain terms it is an Invocation of Divine power. "Quam oblationem, Tu Deus, in omnibus quaesumus, benedictam adscriptam ratam rationabilem acceptabilemque facere dignetis, ut nobis Corpus et Sanguis fiat dilectissimi Filii tui Domini nostri Jesu Christi."

Here is a prayer to GOD to bless the Oblation with the object that it may become—what it is not of itself— the BODY and BLOOD of Christ.

Alexander of Hales, *Summa Theol.* p. iv, qu. 10, memb. 5. After Art. II. "Hic postulatur hostiae benedictae in verum et summum sacrificium transmutatio."

Innocent III., *De Sacrificio Missae* lib. III. c. 12 : "facere benedictam, hoc est transferre in eam hostiam quae est in omnibus benedicta."

Bellarmin (*De Missa* lib. II. cap. 23): "Non oramus pro Eucharistia consecrata sed pro pane et vino consecrando...ut Deus benedicat et sanctificet panem et vinum, ut per eam benedictionem et sanctificationem fiat Corpus et Sanguis Domini."

Florus of Lyons (cited by Le Brun (see below)) of the 9th century is more explicit still : "Quam oblationem

---

[1] e.g. Lorenzana, *Goth. Miss. et Offic. Muzarabici Expositio,* p. 92, citing Benedict XIV.

etc. Oratur Omnipotens Deus, ut oblationem suis sacris altaribus impositam et tantum precibus commendatam, Ipse per virtutem spiritus descendentis ita legitimam et perfectam Eucharistiam perficiat."

And Le Brun (tome I. 160) takes the same view and urges that it is more in conformity with the actual Institution when the Lord first "blessed" the Elements before He declared them His Body and Blood.

For this position and for this plea alleged by Le Brun there is something to be said. It is quite true that the Lord blessed, before He took and declared the Bread His Body and the Cup His Blood. And it is interesting to note that in the Alexandrine type as represented by Bishop Serapion, and S. Mark and the Jacobite S. Mark there is a shorter Invocation in this very place, before the Narrative of Institution, as well as a longer one after it.

Bishop Serapion after the Sanctus has "Full is the heaven...earth of Thy excellent glory, fill also this Sacrifice with Thy power and participation ($\mu\epsilon\tau\alpha\lambda\dot{\eta}$-$\psi\epsilon\omega\varsigma$)." (Edit. Wordsworth, S.P.C.K. p. 62.)

S. Mark: "Full truly is the heaven, etc. Fill, O GOD, also this sacrifice with the blessing which is from Thee through the resting upon it of Thy all holy Spirit." (Brightman, *Liturgies Eastern and Western*, Vol. I. p.132.)

Similarly also in a Gothic Mass (Mabillon XXXVI.) cited above, p. 54.

Hence it may be premised from these instances from such distant quarters, that the earlier place for the Invocation was before the Narrative of Institution

and that the position after it was a later arrangement—
the Latin adhering to the old position and Egyptian
retaining the old, while admitting the new, use.

But the use, which so early became general, of placing
the Invocation after the Narrative of Institution and
in the course of the Prayer of Oblation would seem
preferable. It keeps the two objects of the Eucharist
clearer. It allows the Gifts to be offered as an offering
of Worship and Thanksgiving before asking for their
endowment with Grace for us.

One thing at any rate is clear—the universal
presence of an Invocation.

Now when we turn to our Office, there is nothing expressly asking Divine Intervention to fit the Elements
as vehicles of Grace, either before or after the Narrative
of Institution, except this petition which precedes it:
viz. "Grant that we receiving these Thy creatures of
bread and wine, according to Thy Son's Holy Institution, in remembrance of His death and passion, may be
partakers of His most blessed Body and Blood, Who in
the same night," etc.

There is here no mention of the Holy Ghost, nor
of any consecration or hallowing or blessing to fit the
Elements for their use. There is only a petition for
our reception of the BODY and BLOOD by their means.

This, Bishop Seabury observed, is "the grand fault
of the office," "the deficiency of a more formal oblation
of the Elements and of the Invocation of the Holy
Ghost to sanctify and bless them. The Consecration is
made to consist merely in the Priest's laying his hands

on the Elements and pronouncing 'This is my body,' etc., which words are no consecration at all....The efficacy of Baptism, of Confirmation and of Ordination is ascribed to the Holy Ghost, and His energy is implored for that purpose; and why He should not be invoked in the Consecration of the Eucharist, especially as all[1] the old Liturgies are full to the point, I cannot see." (Dowden's *Annotated Scottish Communion Office*, p. 113.)

Now in the first book of Edward VI. there was an Invocation in this place: viz. immediately before the Narrative of Institution we have "Hear us, O Merciful Father, and with Thy Holy Spirit and Word, vouchsafe to bless and sanctify these Thy creatures of bread and wine that they may be to us the Body and Blood of Thy Son."

This position is identical with the invocatory prayer (Quam Oblationem) in the Latin Rite.

In this form we at once notice the expression, "by Thy Holy Spirit and Word." This probably was not intended for "Logos," but for "formula," i.e. the Narrative of Institution. Because Cranmer in 1551 writing[2] in reply to Gardiner says, "Doth not Irenaeus say plainly 'the chalice mixt and the bread broken after the word of GOD (which you call the words of Consecration), is made Eucharistia of the Body and Blood of Christ'?"

[1] Of course he did not know Bishop Serapion, and he is ignoring the Latin Rite in this remark.

[2] Answer to the "Crafty Cavillation" of Gardiner. Parker Society Ed., p. 266.

Cranmer made appeal to the earliest antiquity, e.g. Justin and Irenaeus, " as the authors nearest to Christ's time and therefore knowing best the truth—they memorised no Invocation and only spoke of the Word "—which he and Gardiner interpreted as " Narrative of Institution."

This interpretation was probably wrong[1], as the recently discovered book of Bishop Serapion has the Invocation of the Word to do what the other forms ask the Holy Spirit to do.

However, such was the view of the time, and it was used to support the Western theory of Consecration by the Narrative of Institution alone. When compiling the first Prayer Book, Cranmer, fresh from his study of Eastern Liturgies, desired to insert an Invocation of the Spirit, and yet not to slight the received view about the sufficiency of the Narrative of Institution. So he brought out a formula of compromise, " Holy Spirit and Word."

After the issue of that book, his opinion underwent a change, probably owing to further acquaintance with Justin and Irenaeus. And through this misinterpretation, he came to think the Invocation of the Holy Spirit non-primitive, and did not recognise the simpler method of Invocation which was primitive, and accordingly deliberately omitted all Invocation from the second book. He formulated instead a prayer, that, as we receive the outward sign, we may then receive the " Inward part or thing signified."

---

[1] And also see above, p. 21 sq. on Justin.

It is a change much to be regretted. Still it is, in part, after the Western manner. For whereas in the Eastern Offices, the petition is that the Elements may by the Spirit's descent be made the BODY and BLOOD of Christ, the Roman and later Gallican only pray that they may "become to us the Body and Blood of Christ."

The East looks at the Sacrament, the West at the recipient.

But the West does ask for the Divine Blessing on the Elements. And even this is omitted in our form. Natural reason tells us that the mere receiving of Bread and Wine cannot make us partakers of the BODY and BLOOD of Christ. No doubt, therefore, this is implied and generally understood when the prayer is used. But a public form of prayer ought to be clear and explicit, so that the simple may gain a clear idea.

Still, when we pray GOD, that receiving the Bread and Wine, we may be partakers of the BODY and BLOOD, we do implicitly pray Him to bring it about. In other words, we beseech Divine intervention to make the Elements the vehicles of the Grace for which they were appointed.

And this implicit petition for Divine intervention with regard to the natural elements, is greatly strengthened by a reference to Christ's Institution—such as is absent from the Latin Office or the First Prayer Book of Edward VI. "Grant that we receiving these Thy creatures of Bread and Wine, *according to Thy Son's Holy Institution*...may be partakers," etc.

We ask GOD to make these Elements serve the purpose for which Christ instituted the Sacrament. We pray that the Elements received in the Rite which Christ appointed may be the means of conveying to us the BODY and BLOOD of Christ.

It is not necessary to specify the instrument, or the method, by which GOD is to accomplish what we ask.

Therefore, the omission of reference to the agency of the Holy Ghost, or the method of benediction, does not invalidate the *sufficiency* of the formula, in which we ask Divine intervention to make the Elements serve the purpose of Christ.   And we can safely look on this petition as indeed a Quasi-Invocation.   And we can follow *Wheatley* in thinking, that "in these words... the sense of the former" (form in the book of 1549) "is still implied, and consequently by these the Elements are now consecrated, and so become the Body and Blood of our Saviour Christ." (*Rational Illustration of B.C.P.* p. 290.)

At the same time, absence of explicit Invocation of the Divine Benediction, and in particular of the Holy Ghost, is a defect, the remedy of which is greatly to be desired.

At least, request should be inserted that GOD would "sanctify and bless" these creatures of bread and wine.   Then we should distinctly invoke GOD to act upon the Elements and make them vehicles of Grace.

Better still, if the request were for the intervention of the Holy Ghost, "the Giver of Life," to make the material elements instinct with spiritual life and power.

The former would conform the rite to primitive precedent. The latter would bring it into line with the general usage of the East, established in distant quarters in the 4th century—a usage born of the deeper spiritual insight that came with passage of time. And such an Invocation of the Spirit would place this Sacrament on the same level as Baptism, where the power of the Holy Spirit is distinctly invoked for the Regeneration of the person to be baptised.

Lastly it would tend to the deepening of faith in the reality of the Sacrament. The Sacrament would be manifestly shown to be a Lifegiving means of Grace, in which God intervenes to fit natural elements for conveying "inward and spiritual Grace." The utility of the Sacrament would be attested. The conception of it would be raised into the region of heavenly activity[1].

ADDITIONAL NOTE ON THE PROVISION FOR A CONSECRATION OF ADDITIONAL ELEMENTS.

The provision for a consecration of further elements is one of the most unsatisfactory features in our Office.

The Rubric runs, "if the consecrated Bread and Wine be all spent before all have Communicated, the Priest is to Consecrate more according to the form before prescribed; beginning at [Our Saviour Christ

[1] The question of an amended position for the Invocation will be dealt with in the next chapter.

in the same night, etc.] for the blessing of the Bread;
and at [Likewise after Supper, etc.] for the blessing of
the Cup."

If some prayer for the intervention of the Divine
Power is necessary for the original Consecration, surely
it is so for a second.

This defect was noticed by Wheatley long ago.
"The words of Institution are the only words re-
corded....But then...the Evangelists tell us, that He
gave thanks and blessed the Bread and Wine; and this
sure must have been done in other words than those
which He spake at the delivery of them to His disciples;
for blessing and thanksgiving must be performed by
some words addressed to GOD, and not by any words
addressed to man....And therefore, I humbly presume,
that if the minister should at the consecration of fresh
elements, after the others are spent, repeat again the
whole form of Consecration or at least from those words
'Hear us, O merciful Father,' etc., he would answer the
end of the rubric, which seems only to require the latter
part." (*Rational Illustration of B.C.P.* p. 291 and sq.)

And of this petition, which he thinks necessary here,
he said, "the sense of the former" (Invocation of 1549)
"is still implied, and consequently by these the Elements
are now Consecrated, and so become the Body and
Blood of Our Saviour Christ" (*op. cit.* p. 290).

In accordance with this same feeling, the Scottish
Office and the American require the use of the full
consecratory form, viz. the Commemoration of Redemption, of the Institution, and the Oblation and Invocation.

The *whole* form[1] is used even when only one species has failed.

In early times the failure of either species was a rare occurrence if it ever happened. The habit of communicating was general and regular—hence the numbers at the celebrations would be fairly constant. Besides it was the practice to consecrate in large quantities, so as to always have large quantities remaining for reservation, and, at one time, for people to take away and communicate themselves at home.

An early practice, for the provision of extra wine, was to add further wine to the remains in the nearly spent cup, and to regard the contact and mingling of the addition with the remains of the consecrated wine as of itself effecting consecration. Any failure of the species of bread was provided against by sub-division of the breads originally consecrated.

In the West, along with the growth of irregularity and infrequency of communicating, came the custom of Communion in one kind.

The Reformation therefore, with the restoration of the Cup to the laity, brought a contingency which had never arisen for centuries.

The Order of Communion of 1548 provided for sub-division of the breads "in two pieces at the least, or more, by the discretion of the minister," in case of the

[1] The use of the full form involves the consecration of both species in all cases. And the recently Revised Scottish Rubric says so *totidem verbis*: "If the consecrated Bread or Wine be all spent...the Presbyter is to consecrate more *in both kinds,*" etc.

bread falling short: and for our present method in the case of the failure of the wine.

In 1549 and subsequent editions of our Office no provision was made for a second consecration. Priests were left to the guidance of custom.

Puritan neglect necessitated definite direction, and in 1662 our present Rubric was inserted. It directs a similar method for supplying the failure of bread or of wine: viz. the recitation of the part of the Narrative of Institution referring to the particular species that had fallen short.

This was following the later mediaeval precedent in the event of an omission to put wine into the chalice at the Offertory.

That mediaeval practice was based on the theory current in the West, that consecration is effected by the taking of the Elements by the priest in imitation of Christ, and as His representative, and by the saying of the words over them which Christ said at the Institution. But to this, Wheatley's objection seems unanswerable. Consecration could not be effected by Christ's command to men, much less by the recitation of that command.

There must be prayer to GOD to bless and give spiritual efficacy.

In this instance of a second consecration, it may be argued that the prayer of Invocation, or quasi-Invocation said at the consecration proper, has efficacy for all the bread or wine that shall be required during the celebration; and the words of Institution set apart and bring under its efficacy.

There is a great deal to be said for this theory. But there is no such idea conveyed to ordinary people. It gives the impression, on which it undoubtedly was based, that the words of Institution effect consecration.

This theory of consecration has had general acceptance in the West since the days of the Schoolmen. This practice is after the long-standing method of the West. Therefore we can rest on this general belief and practice, and on the idea of the extension of the prayer at the main consecration.

Still an improvement is devoutly to be wished. At least Wheatley's suggestion should be followed, and the quasi-Invocation before the Narrative of Institution said.

If, and when, the much to be desired conforming of our Office to the Scottish model is attained, some different method would be required.

Now the Scottish and American method seems to involve a second celebration, in the recitation of the Verbal Oblation, and the consecration of both species. There can surely be only one celebration—one offering of the memorial in the one service. And the consecration of extra elements is not for the purposes of making memorial to GOD—that has been done, and all present have taken part in that—but for the Communion of more worshippers. What is wanted, it seems, is the use of either Word of Institution, and the Invocation, omitting mention of the element of which no fresh supply is needed.

This would be short and simple, and yet would make it plain that prayer for the intervention of Divine

Power, and not recitation of the Word of Institution, after the manner of a charm, gives the spiritual efficacy to the Elements.

NOTE. Strictly, there should first be a verbal offering of the element, as at the Offertory was done for the original elements—but the placing on the Altar has been held sufficient offering of itself, without accompanying words.

CHAPTER IX

THE SEPARATION OF THE EUCHARISTIC ACT FROM
THE COMMEMORATION OF THE INSTITUTION,
AND THE ABSENCE OF THANKSGIVING FOR RE-
DEMPTION

THE very name Eucharist indicates Praise as the
primary object of the service.

It was after that "He had given thanks" over the
bread and wine that the Saviour brake and distributed
the Bread, and gave the Cup. So Justin says, "bread
and a cup of water and wine are brought to him who
presides over the brethren. And he, taking it, sends
up praise and glory to the Father of all....And he
makes at great length a thanksgiving, for that we have
been counted worthy to receive these gifts from GOD....

"After he who presides has given thanks, and all the
people have said Amen, those...deacons give to every
one...to partake." (*Ap.* I. c. LXV. § 3.)

And the regular and primitive method, as seen in
the Eastern and Gallican Liturgies, was for the Eucharistic Act (Sursum Corda, Preface (as we call it)
and Sanctus) to lead on through the Thankful

Commemoration of Creation and Redemption to the Narrative of Institution[1].

The idea was, that the worshippers met to offer Thanksgiving and Worship to the Giver and Lord of all—along with the offering to Him of material Gifts, which the Son had appointed. And, therefore, adoration in general terms was succeeded by thankful commemoration of Redemption, and of the Institution of the "perpetual memory" thereof, and by request for the acceptance of the same. But in our Office we find the sequence broken, and the thanksgiving for Redemption absent.

§ 1.   *The Sequence is broken.*

The crown of the solemnity of Thanksgiving and Worship is reached in the Sanctus, in which the song of earthly worship is mingled with that of the worship of the Heavenly Host.

Then there is a break.

(*a*)   A prayer is inserted, of humiliation, and petition for grace to receive rightly, viz. the "Prayer of Humble Access."

(β)   After a collect-like address a petition follows, that the reception of the Elements may bring participation in the BODY and BLOOD of Christ (this is a quasi-Invocation).

Then the Narrative of Institution.

[1] In Bishop Serapion's Liturgy (ed. Wordsworth, p. 62) there is no thanksgiving for Redemption here, and in S. Mark (Brightman, *Liturgies Eastern and Western*, Vol. I. p. 132) and the Coptic only a slight allusion (*ibid*. p. 176).

The thought is brought down from the Adoration of the Most High to the benefit of ourselves.

It is true that in the Latin Rite, and in our Office of 1549, there is an interruption in this place. But in the Office of 1549 it was for Intercession and definite Invocation. And in the Latin Office it was, to ask acceptance of the Oblation (Te Igitur), to make Intercession (Memento), to Commemorate the Saints (Communicantes), to plead the Oblation (Hanc Oblationem), and to address an Invocation to the Most High.

In the book, too, of Bishop Serapion[1], S. Mark[2] and the Coptic[3], the sequence of praise is broken by an Invocation.

In all these, however, the interruption continues to fix the thought on the Heavenly Altar, whereas ours turns it away to the individual benefit accruing from right reception.

(γ) We have, indeed, seen that the petition prefixed immediately to the Narrative of Institution may be reasonably taken for a quasi-Invocation.

On this interpretation, our Office in regard to this petition is not alone, but has the company of Alexandrine, Latin and Gothic examples.

But the usage is open in all these instances to two objections:

(i) It tends to make the object of Christ's Institution, of which the account is given, appear as solely for

---

[1] Ed. Wordsworth, p. 62.

[2] Brightman's *Liturgies Eastern and Western*, Vol. I. p. 132.

[3] *Ibid.* p. 176.

the conveyance of Grace to us, instead of also, and chiefly, for the presentation by us of His memorial to GOD.

(ii)   It separates the setting of the Gifts apart for GOD'S service, and so offering them to Him, from the Eucharistic Act, and thus obscures the fact of their being Gifts of Worship and Praise, following the words of Praise.

The rationale of the whole sacred transaction is: Praise is offered in words, and then in act by these Gifts.   The natural Gifts are palpable tokens of tribute and thanksgiving.   Words have been uttered, now something is offered.

And besides, they are offered not only in themselves, as a sort of firstfruits of His creatures, but by their means Christ is Offered, the "one true pure immortal Sacrifice" of Christ is presented.

It is a memorial of Him.   This is the centre and kernel of the whole transaction.   Prayer and praise offered in the course of the Office, are offered in conjunction with the ONE Offering of Christ here pleaded.

It is surely a defect, and a grave defect, that by any severance, the conjunction of the Offering of Praise with the Oblation of Christ effected at the representation of the Institution, should be obscured.

The objections are much minimised in the cases of the Alexandrine family, where the Invocation intervening is a definitely worded petition for Divine intervention, and there is no other interruption.

But in our Office the objections are greatly accentuated by the vagueness of the quasi-Invocation, which *seems* to make it but a prayer for ourselves: and further exaggerated by the interjection of the " Prayer of Humble Access."

This not only by its very presence produces a distinct severance, and makes the Narrative of Institution an adjunct of a prayer, instead of praise; but its very character introduces a thought alien to its position. It solely has regard to receiving. There is no mention of unworthiness to present any Offering to GOD. Yet this is the chief object of the service and the chief purpose and effect of the Commemoration of the Institution. Beautiful as the prayer is, it is incongruous where it is now placed. It was written to precede the actual Communion, and for that place alone it is suitable. To that place it should be restored, and so the current of Praise could flow on, and find its climax and final expression in the Oblation made in the Commemoration of the Institution.

It is of course true that the Office is one whole, as a whole it is offered to GOD and as a whole it is regarded and accepted by Him. It is true, also, that the instructed know that all prayers and Praise are offered in connection with the Offering of Christ, made at the Commemoration of the Institution.

But in a solemn and premeditated form of Office, seemliness and sequence should not be thus violated. In any Office for public use, everything should be so arranged as to convey naturally and simply to the uninstructed the idea and principle of the Office.

The Presentation of Praise and Worship by the

Gifts, and in connection with the Offering of Christ presented to the Most High in the solemn imitation of Christ's Institution, and afterwards in set phrases of Oblation, should stand out distinct and clear as the first and chief object of the service, quite independently of the individual's subsequent receiving of Sacramental Grace.

§ 2. *The Absence of Thanksgiving for Redemption.*

We must now consider the fact that in our Office, the Eucharistic Act ends with the Adoring Song for Creation, and includes no Thanksgiving for Redemption.

The general method[1] of the ancient Liturgies was to lead up to the Commemoration of the Institution, immediately from Thanksgiving for the Incarnation and Saving Life and Death of our Redeemer.

The Angels, and all creation, can join in adoration for creation, but man has special call for it in the Redemption.

For example, the "Clementine" (Brightman, *Liturgies Eastern and Western*, Vol. I. pp. 19 and 20):

" For Holy indeed art Thou. And All-Holy the Highest and most Exalted for ever. And Holy is also Thine Only Begotten Son...Who...did not overlook the Lost Race of men, but...was pleased Himself...the Creator to become Man...and propitiated Thee....He

[1] The exceptions are the Latin Rite and Bishop Serapion's where there is no thanksgiving for the Incarnation and Redemption ; and S. Mark and the Coptic have only a brief allusion.

was born...Living among men holily...was nailed to the Cross...died...rose again...was taken up into heaven and was set at Thy right Hand....

"Wherefore we having in remembrance the things which He suffered...give thanks unto Thee...and fulfil His injunction. For He in the same night," etc.

But in our Office there is no such Thanksgiving.

There is an acknowledgement of GOD'S "tender mercy in giving His Son to suffer death" for our Redemption, but it is an acknowledgement by way of bare statement, and not in terms of thanksgiving.

No doubt, this acknowledgement, that the Saving Death is alone the result of GOD'S tender mercy to man, is sufficient.

And if there were no interruption between it and the Sanctus, it might have been argued, that it was a specific mention of a particular ground for the general Thanksgiving and Praise which had just been rendered. But it is cut off by the interpolated prayer, and is in fàct only an introductory statement in a prayer, which is a quasi-Invocation—asking Him to make the natural elements conveyances of Christ's BODY and BLOOD.

In so far as there is this acknowledgement of "GOD'S Tender Mercy" in giving His Son, our Office is superior to the Latin and Bishop Serapion's Office, which have no allusion at all to Redeeming love at this point. And the reference in this brief fashion is not so very unlike the brief and general reference to Redemption in S. Mark and the Coptic.

S. Mark has, after the Sanctus—"For full, truly, is

the heaven and the earth of Thy holy glory through
the manifestation of our Lord and GOD and Saviour
Jesus Christ." (Brightman, *Liturgies Eastern and
Western*, Vol. I. p. 132.)

The Coptic—"Truly heaven and earth are full of
Thine Holy Glory, through Thine only begotten Son our
Lord, and our GOD, and our Saviour and the King of us
all, Jesus Christ." (*Ibid.* p. 176.)

But in these instances, it is a continuation of the
Praise of the Sanctus, and a definite, separate sentence.
In our Office, it is divided from the Eucharistic Act by
a prayer of humiliation, and is, in fact, but an "obiter
dictum" introductory to the prayer following. We hurry
from one prayer for ourselves to another. Reference to
benefit received, so curt and so hurried over, were
hardly conformed to canons of courtesy between man
and man. How can we describe it, when such inestimable Benefit is in question, and the Benefactor is the
Most High?

Surely, in a public Office, feelings ought not to be
assumed, but find adequate expression in words. The
requirements of bare sufficiency may be met in this
reference, but the measure of their treatment is
defective.

CHAPTER X

THE OMISSION, OR TRANSFERENCE OF THE GREAT OBLATION, AND ITS FORM

THE normal feature of all the chief Liturgies is a solemn petition for the acceptance of our Memorial, immediately after the Commemoration of the Institution.

For example, in the "*Clementine*": "For as oft as ye eat, etc.

"Wherefore...we offer unto Thee...this bread and this cup...and we beseech Thee...accept." (Brightman, *Liturgies Eastern and Western*, Vol. I. pp. 20–21.)

In *S. James*: "For as oft as ye eat, etc.

"We, therefore...offer to Thee this tremendous and unbloody sacrifice, beseeching Thee that Thou shouldest not deal with us after our sins," etc. (*Ibid.* pp. 52–53.)

In the *Missale Gothicum*: "For as oft, etc.

"We keeping, O Lord, these institutions and precepts, pray Thee supplicatingly, that Thou wouldest vouchsafe to accept this Sacrifice...." Mabillon VIII. *Gothic Mass.*

In the *Latin use*: "For as oft, etc.

"Wherefore we...do offer...a pure Host...the cup of eternal Salvation. Whereon...do Thou be pleased to look down and to accept them," etc.

In 1*st Prayer Book of Edward VI.*: "For as oft, etc.

"Wherefore...we do celebrate and make here the memorial...desiring Thy Fatherly Goodness to accept this our sacrifice," etc.

But when we approach our *present Office*, we find, on the conclusion of the Narrative of Institution, no such solemn offering or petition that our memorial may be accepted. But, after the Communion and Lord's Prayer, we do find what was the Prayer of Oblation in the 1st Book of Edward VI., with some modifications.

This change, says Bishop Horsley, was "made to humour the Calvinists, much for the worse." (Letter to Rev. J. Skinner quoted in Bishop Dowden's *Annotated Scottish Communion Office*, p. 106.) And Thorndike (*Just Weights*, ch. xx.) says, "That Memorial or prayer of Oblation is certainly more proper there (i.e. immediately after the Consecration Prayer) than after the Communion."

Bishop Cosin (*Works* v. 114) vainly tried in 1662 to procure the restoration of the Prayer to its former position. And he justified his effort:

(i) By alleging that the constant practice of his "master" (Bishop Overall) was always to say it after the Consecration Prayer, in spite of its printed position.

(ii) By urging that "we ought first to send up Christ to God, and then He will send Him down to us."

I. In these old Divines, we have a controversion of the opinion sometimes expressed in these days that the Prayer after the Lord's Prayer is no Prayer of Oblation. *They* thought so, living near the time of the change of its position. They held that it was only a question of position, the substantial identity and object of the prayer being the same. What was wanted—they said— was not a new prayer of Oblation, but a restoration of the old to its true and original place. They did not consider the "*form*" of the offering, curtailed as it is, in this prayer as destructive of its identity with the Oblation of Edward VI.'s First Book, or of its necessary constitution as a Prayer of Oblation.

The form of our Prayer is as follows: "Almighty... we entirely desire Thy Fatherly goodness mercifully to accept this our sacrifice of praise and thanksgiving; most humbly beseeching Thee to grant, that by the Merits and Death of Thy Son Jesus Christ and through faith in His blood, we and all Thy whole Church may obtain remission of our sins and all other benefits of His passion."

Now in 1549 the Prayer began, "Wherefore, O Lord and Heavenly Father, according to the Institution of Thy dearly beloved Son, Our Saviour Jesus Christ, we Thy humble servants do celebrate and make here before Thy divine Majesty, with these Thy holy Gifts ["which we now offer unto Thee[1]"], the memorial which Thy Son had willed ["commanded"] us to make; having

[1] The variations of the Scottish and American form are indicated within [ ].

in remembrance His Blessed Passion ["and precious death"], Mighty Resurrection and glorious Ascension rendering unto Thee most hearty thanks for the innumerable benefits procured unto us by the same ["and ...(Invocation). And we earnestly desire"], earnestly desiring thy Fatherly goodness," etc.

This contains a more solemn act of offering and request for acceptance. It also presents a fuller and richer view of the work of Christ, after the manner of the old Liturgies. They did not confine it to the Death, but included the Resurrection and Ascension.

For example—the "Clementine" (Brightman, *Liturgies Eastern and Western*, Vol. I. pp. 20, 21):

"Remembering therefore His Passion and Death and Resurrection and Ascension into heaven and His future Second Coming, in which He is coming to judge ...we offer...this bread and this cup...look favourably on these gifts lying before Thee," etc.

S. James (Brightman, *op. cit.* p. 52):

"Remembering therefore, even we the sinners, His lifegiving Sufferings, the Saving Cross, and Death, and Burial, and the Rising again the third day from the dead, and the Ascension into heaven, and Session at the right hand of Thee, the GOD and Father, and His Second Glorious and dreadful Coming, when He comes with glory to judge...spare us, O Lord our GOD, and the rather according to His Compassion, we offer to Thee, O Lord, this fearful and unbloody Sacrifice...."

So, in substance, all the Eastern Liturgies.

The Gallican form I have already quoted from the Gothic Missal…"we pray Thee vouchsafe to accept… this Sacrifice."

The Roman Canon, as quoted in the work *De Sacramentis* of the Pseudo-Ambrose—a work of a date near 400—has:

"Therefore mindful of His most glorious Passion and Resurrection from Hades and Ascension into Heaven, we offer this immaculate host, this holy bread and cup of eternal life…." (*De Sacram.* IV. 5, Migne, *Pat. Lat.* Vol. XVI. p. 443.)

Similarly the later Canon, only in expanded phrasing.

But the mediaeval schoolmen made the Commemoration to consist in the Memorial of the Passion: e.g. S. Peter of Cluny (died 1156) says, "If it is asked, why it is the presentation of His Death, rather than of His Resurrection or Ascension, the answer is that by His Death He restored Life to the dead and saved the world." *P. L.* CLXXXIX. 813.

Peter Lombard: "On the Cross Christ died once, and there was He offered in Himself; in the Sacrament He is offered daily, because in the Sacrament there is the Commemoration of that which was done once" (IV. xii. 7). S. Thomas Aquinas *passim*, but e.g. S. T. LXXIII. 4, "It is called a Sacrifice in so far as it represents the Passion itself of Christ."

So that our form, whether intentionally or not, is a following of the schoolmen rather than of the Liturgies and the old and primitive teachers.

All reference to the glorified consummation of Christ's

S. 6

work is omitted, and all that we have is, "we entirely desire Thy Fatherly goodness to accept this our Sacrifice of praise and thanksgiving, humbly beseeching Thee to grant that by the merits and death of Thy Son," etc.

The expression "Sacrifice of praise and thanksgiving" is derived from the concluding part of the Intercession which followed the Oblation in the Latin Canon. "Remember Thy servants...who are offering unto Thee this Sacrifice of praise."

The phrase "Sacrifice of thanksgiving" occurs in the Vulgate of Lev. vii. 13 "sacrificium gratiarum" and in LXX θυσία αἰνέσεως as a description of the meat offering.

It does not mean that the Sacrifice is one consisting of "praise and thanksgiving" but that this is the character of the Sacrifice. So it was understood at the time.

It was the precise term exacted by the mediaeval party from Shaxton, Bishop of Salisbury in 1546, of the "oblation and action" of the Priest in the Mass as a proof of his repudiation of Protestant Doctrine [1]." So the Marian Bishop Watson (in *Wholesome and Catholic Doctrine*, fol. lxxviii. *a*) says: "The Church offers Christ Her Head to GOD the Father as a worthy sacrifice of praise and thanks." And Ridley: "Our unbloody sacrifice of the Church is none other than the sacrifice of praise and thanksgiving, than a commemoration, a showing forth, and a sacramental representation of that one bloody Sacrifice offered up once for all" (*Works*, pp. 210–11).

[1] Burnet, *History of the Reformation*, Vol. i. part 2, p. 399.

And Bellarmine says on this phrase in the Canon: "Sacrifice of praise, because by it GOD is greatly praised." (*De Missâ* Lib. II. c. 21.) "Sacrifice of praise" is common, in fact, to Gallican and Eastern Liturgies.

The addition of "and thanksgiving" is to amplify the description and probably to embody the phrase of Leviticus vii. 13.

The expression was recognised and taken to describe the Oblation of Christ in the Eucharist, and the phrase "Sacrifice of praise" had long been in use in the old Canon in this sense. And in the absence of any intimation of different use, it must be taken in the same sense here. This conclusion is strengthened by the succeeding petition: "most humbly beseeching Thee to grant that by the merits and death of Thy Son...we ...may obtain remission of sins and all other benefits of His Passion."

Here we have a participial clause dependent on what precedes. Such a construction explains and defines. (Compare "Go ye, make disciples...baptising them," etc. The participle explains how the disciples were to be made such.) The "Sacrifice of praise and thanksgiving" is the pleading of Christ's merits and Death. Otherwise there is a failure of sequence in the logic and construction of the Prayer.

And the petition for remission is after the general manner of the ancient prayers of Oblation.

Regretting, as we must, the absence of richer and more detailed pleading of Christ's Life and Work, past and present, for us, we cannot doubt that there is a definite offering of the "Memorial" which Christ ordained, and request for the acceptance of His Redemptive work on behalf of ourselves and the whole Church.

However defective, it is sufficient. The only grave fault about the prayer is its position—apart from the Narrative of Institution.

II. But before proceeding to reflect on the position, we must notice a special feature of this prayer of Oblation. "And here we offer and present unto Thee, O Lord, ourselves, our souls and bodies, to be a reasonable, holy, and lively sacrifice unto Thee."

It was introduced in 1549.

There was a direction in the *Lay Folks' Mass Book* (ed. Canon Simmons p. 233) in use, "When the Priest doth take the chalice and hold it...offer yourself to Him again, both soul and body." And as the cup was withholden from the Laity, this reference was to the time of Consecration and Offering. When the Priest offers the Oblation of Christ, then each worshipper must offer himself. This accords with the primal and essential rationale of sacrifice. Sacrifice of a victim symbolised the offering of self. Without the offering of self, the external and symbolical offering was worthless. This is an eternal law of human nature. The law holds in common intercourse with one another. We attach no value, or but little, to a gift which, we have reason to feel sure, does not really represent the genuine feelings of love and regard of the giver towards us. And on the other hand we value most highly

even the trifling gift which we know is accompanied
by the sincere devotion of the giver.

Obviously there must be the self-oblation of the
worshippers, if the Oblation is to be accepted for them.
But our Office is the only one which. gives to this
definite expression in this connection.

The introduction was due probably, in part, to the
characteristic object of the Reformers to emphasise the
individual's obligation of real personal oblation, to the
direction of the old popular manual (*Lay Folks' Mass
Book*) then current, to a prayer in the Leonine Sacramentary, and to the great influence of the writings of
S. Augustine.

The prayer in the Leonine Sacramentary was "that
GOD would propitiously sanctify the Church's gifts, and,
accepting the oblation of their spiritual sacrifice, would
make the worshippers themselves an eternal offering to
Him." (*P. L.* LV. 40.)

S. Augustine dwelt much on the point which I have
been making, and expressed it in terms of the special
relationship between us and Christ.

Christ and we are not separate entities like the old
sacrifice and the offerer. We are one with Christ, as
His members. The Offering, therefore, of Christ by
His members involves the offering of themselves.

So in *De Civ. Dei* L. x. c. xix. "In offering sacrifice,
we should know that the visible sacrifice is to be
offered to no other than Him, whose invisible sacrifice
we ought to be in our hearts." And in Sermon cclxxii.
on 1 Cor. x. 16–7 he writes: "How is the bread His

body? and the cup or what it contains, how is it His blood? Those, brethren, are therefore called Sacraments, because in them one thing is seen, one thing is understood; what is seen has a corporal appearance, what is understood has spiritual fruit (effect). If you wish therefore to understand the Body of Christ, hear the Apostle saying to the faithful, ' Ye are the body of Christ and members of it.' If therefore ye are the body of Christ and members of it, the mystery of yourselves is placed on the Lord's Table; the mystery of yourselves you receive. To that which ye are, ye respond Amen, and by responding ye write it over again. For you hear ' the BODY of Christ' and you respond Amen: be the member of Christ's body, that your Amen may be true. Why is It then in the bread?...let us hear the Apostle in the same place, who, when he was speaking of that Sacrament, says, ' Because we are one bread, we being many are one body.' Understand and rejoice....Be what ye see and take what ye are."

And in Sermon ccxxvii. " If you have received well, you are that which you have received." Also in *De Civ. Dei*, x. 6, " This is the Sacrifice of Christians: ' the many one body in Christ.' Which also the Church celebrates in the Sacrament of the altar, familiar to the faithful, where it is shown to her that in this thing which she offers, she herself is offered."

S. Clement of Alexandria had dwelt on the Christian Sacrifice of devotion and holy living, but had not touched on the identification between that and the Offering of Christ in the Eucharist. *Strom.* VII. vi. 31–2, iii. 14.

Later S. Gregory followed in the steps of S. Augustine, e.g. *Dial.* IV. 59, 60, " We must offer ourselves to GOD with a penitent heart, because we who celebrate the mysteries of the Passion of the Lord are bound to imitate the rite which we perform. Then will it be really a sacrifice to GOD on our behalf, when we have made ourselves a sacrifice."

And later still Ratramn in *De Corp. et Sang. Dom.* LXXIII. 4, " In the bread there is a figure not only of the Body of Christ, but also of the body of the people believing in Him....As that bread is taken to be the Body of Christ in a mystery, so also in a mystery the members of the people believing in Christ are signified."

Because of the oneness of the members with Christ, there is a oneness with the Sacrament of His BODY and BLOOD : there is a oneness between the worshipper and the Sacrament which is received and offered.

They are mystically one with the Oblation, and mystically offered in it. That should be consciously realised and felt by each worshipper. Therefore it is most appropriate that it should find expression. In this our Office has a peculiar merit. We offer the Memorial of Christ, and then offer ourselves in terms reminiscent of phrases in Hermann's *Consultatio* in the Chapter " of Holy Oblations" published in 1547 in an English edition.

III.   Now let us return to the question of position.

(1)   The present position—separated from the Narrative of Institution—is a grave defect.

It is contrary to general precedent and to the fitness of things.

After the Commemoration of Redemption and Institution—narrating what Christ did, how He appointed this "perpetual memory," and what He did when He appointed it—the natural sequence is to ask for the acceptance of our Memorial and to plead it for its benefits.

This is the normal arrangement, though in the Liturgy of Malabar it precedes the Consecration. And in the Egyptian Offices (e.g. S. Mark[1] and the Coptic[2]) there is no solemn offering or prayer for acceptance, but a statement "we have set forth," i.e. in the Consecration prayer, in which Commemoration is made of the Institution.

Still these are exceptions to the general recognition that fitness requires that, after doing what Christ ordained, we should ask for our Offering to be accepted.

So placed, the sequence of ideas would be simple and obvious to the unlearned. Now the connection with the Consecration prayer is obscured by this separation. The mind is diverted from what Christ did, to what the worshipper is to receive, the Sacramental Gifts. The attention is removed from the presentation of the Memorial, and it is difficult to take up the thought of it again.

And out of connection with the Consecration prayer, the reference to self-oblation is apt to assume

---

[1] Brightman, *Liturgies Eastern and Western*, Vol. i. p. 133.

[2] *Ibid.* p. 178. This probably is, as we have suggested before in a note on Chapter vii., due to an older idea that the Offering took place at the Offertory (see p. 47 above and also p. 20).

a wrong proportion. The Offering which Christ ordained, and which we meet to make, is the Memorial
of Himself. The oblation of ourselves may be made at
any time and is merely a moral requirement and a
mystical application of an Objective Reality to ourselves. It is a necessary requisite. The mention of it
is a unique excellence of our Office. But we need to
guard against any misconception. The Offering in the
Eucharist is Christ. The offering of ourselves is only
a corollary. The mention of this offering of ourselves
makes the restoration of the prayer to its original
connection with the Prayer of Consecration more than
ever imperative. Placed there, all is plain, and all
assumes its right proportion. We do what Christ
ordained, and we ask acceptance of this Memorial of
Him—the one Offering—and then, because of that, and
along with that, we offer ourselves.

(2) Further, the present position of the prayer is
unsuitable because of this self-oblation and the petition
following it.

(a) It makes the Oblation of the worshipper after
Reception. No doubt the great motive of Cranmer
and the Reformers was to encourage Communion
and discourage non-communicating attendance at the
Memorial. And the rationale of the change of structure
which he made in 1552 may well be that, in view of
the necessity of the self-oblation of the worshippers,
they should first Communicate and be incorporated
afresh into Christ who is offered to the Father. But
this overlooks the fact of the already existing " Member-

ship in Christ" which is an abiding state effected by Baptism. The Christian is already in union with Christ, and on the ground of this in a position to join the personal oblation of himself with the Oblation of Christ which he shares in pleading. The present position of this Oblation robs the Communicant of the benefit of the spiritual effort of oblation in producing the fittest frame of mind for Receiving.

And the connection of this self-oblation is definite in the prayer. It is a preliminary to a petition for the Benefits of the Sacrament. "Here we offer...ourselves...humbly beseeching Thee that all we...may be fulfilled," etc.

The object, therefore, of this self-oblation, as originally conceived and placed in the former book of 1549, was as a motive and stimulus to subsequent right reception.

And this is most in accord with the fitness of things. For if a self-oblation of gratitude is due after, a self-oblation of wholehearted surrender and waiting on God before, receiving His Gift are an absolute essential. This should find formal and verbal expression *before* the receiving of the Sacrament of Grace.

(β) It prays that those who have received may be filled with Grace. But if the Sacramental Elements are "efficacious signs," the Grace of the Sacrament has been already received. It may be allowable to pray after reception (as in the Confirmation Service), that the Grace received "may ever remain." It is hardly true to pray after receiving, to be filled as if nothing had been received. It may indeed be urged that the Grace prayed for is the "virtus sacramenti," not the "res sacramenti." But this is using an old prayer in a new sense. For the whole prayer preceded Communion in 1549, and this petition ran, "whosoever shall be partakers of this Holy Communion may worthily receive the most Blessed Body and Blood of Thy Son Jesus Christ and be fulfilled with Thy grace and heavenly benediction." This prayer is but a slight variant of one in the old Canon, viz. "as many as, by this partaking of the altar, shall have received the most sacred Body and Blood of Thy Son, may be fulfilled with all heavenly benediction and grace." (Te Igitur.)

It is one thing to pray so to receive as to have the "benefits," another, after receiving, that having received we may enjoy the benefits. In the one case, it is a prayer for preparation for right reception. In our prayer, it is prayer for a change of disposition, that what has been received may become operative.

Such a prayer has scarcely a fit place anywhere, since it can hardly be imagined that reception in an unprepared state would be contemplated and provided for in compilation of liturgical forms. The very contents therefore of the prayer seem to show the inappropriateness of its present position.

Reviewing the whole we see that the position of the prayer, and the terms of the Oblation, may well be regarded as defects, and specially the former.

At the same time, we may reflect that the Office is one entity, and position in any part of it is in connection with the Central Act of Consecration. And indeed while the Prayer is being said, the Sacramental Elements left over are still upon the altar. The "Sacrifice of praise and thanksgiving" does describe the Offering of Christ which He appointed and the mention of His death alone is not without parallel—and His death was the prime cause of Redemption.

There can be, therefore, no ground for judging that there is in our Office any "*insufficiency*" of form asking acceptance of the Oblation of Christ. No supplementing of the Office by the use of the form of Oblation from the old Rite is justified.

Yet, at the same time, it is most desirable that the terms of the Oblation should be enriched and the position after the Narrative of Institution restored. This restoration would improve the sequence and order-liness of arrangement, and conduce to greater edification. And this consideration is greatly enhanced by the special feature of this prayer, which makes the oblation of our-selves the climax of the Oblation.

For so restored, there would be given not merely a clearer idea of what the Offering in the Eucharist is, not merely a clearer conception of the connection of this Oblatory form with the Consecration prayer, not merely in consequence more intelligent participation in the Service, but also a spiritual motive would be supplied to the intending Communicant.

CHAPTER XI

THE POSITION OF THE COMMUNICANTS' PREPARATION

THE solemnity of the act of Communion would suggest of itself some devotions for the preparation of the Communicants. Their sinfulness would crave forgiveness and their unworthiness mercy. Accordingly we find this natural feeling given voice in all Liturgies.

(1)   In all the *Eastern Liturgies* except the Clementine the Lord's Prayer is given a place for this end, with a prefatory or supplementary supplication or both.

And in all, there is also the Inclination or " Prayer of Humble Access," except in the Nestorian and in the account of S. Cyril.

All is introduced by a Blessing.   And in every case there is no more than the Elevation or the Elevation and Manual Acts between this preparation and the Communion.

The Clementine (Brightman, *Liturgies Eastern and Western*, Vol. I. pp. 23 and sq.) has, after the Intercession, a Blessing, the Inclination, Elevation, Communion.

The Nestorian (Brightman, *op. cit.* p. 293 and sq.) has, in the same place, a Blessing, Lord's Prayer only,

with preface and supplement (the Embolismus), in two
alternate versions, (1) said quietly and (2) aloud, then
the Elevation and Communion. But the *general
manner* was a Blessing, then the Priest says privately
a prayer to be made worthy and then aloud the Lord's
Prayer with a short preface and Embolismus and
Inclination, then the Elevation and Manual Acts and
Communion.

There is the slight variation from this in S. James
(Brightman, *op. cit.* p. 58 and sq.) of placing the Blessing
last, after the Inclination, instead of first: and in
S. Mark and the Coptic there is no Blessing. (Brightman, *op. cit.* pp. 135 and sq. and p. 182.)

(2) In the *Western Liturgies* there is the Lord's
Prayer with a short preface and Embolismus. There is
no Inclination. But the Mozarabic has an exhortation
to faith in its "bidding" of the Nicene Creed, and
a Benediction preceded by a charge to the worshippers
to humble themselves for it. And since the 8th century
the Roman has had two Collects immediately before
Communion.

The greatness of the Sacrament was always realised
and an endeavour was made in all Liturgies to prepare
the Communicants to receive. Whether by the Lord's
Prayer[1] alone or with the addition of "Inclination,"

[1] The "Rationale," drawn up soon after the King's Book, *c.* 1543,
says: "The Priest then to the intent, he may the more worthily
receive the blessed BODY and BLOOD of Christ, both to the comfort
and strength as well of him as well as of them that be present, saith
the Pater Noster."

Creed, and Benediction, it was sought to move to humility, repentance and faith.

Between this preparation and Communion the Elevation and Manual Acts made no interruption. As we shall see the original Elevation was an incentive to moral effort to be holy. The Manual Acts were a symbolical preparation of the Elements for the Communicants.

The rationale of the scheme was first to complete the duty to GOD in the Praise and Oblation and Intercession, and then for the intending Communicants to prepare themselves to Receive.

In the First Prayer Book of Edward the Sixth, after the Oblation, came the Lord's Prayer and Embolismus after the ancient manner. Then followed our Invitation, Confession, Absolution, Comfortable Words and Prayer of Humble Access. And after that came the Communion.

This was all of admirable conception: a reminder of the requisites for Communion, confession of sin and a prayer humbly begging to rightly receive, and in the Absolution and Comfortable Words, assurance of pardon, mercy and favour.

Now turn to our Office and we find this preparation divided and the sundered parts moved to fresh places. The Invitation, Confession, Absolution and Comfortable Words are put back and placed before the Eucharistic Act, and the Prayer of Humble Access is put in front of the Prayer of Consecration. The Lord's Prayer with the Embolismus is omitted altogether. This constitutes a grave defect in our Office.

It creates incongruity and a void.

The new positions of these parts of the Communicants' preparation are unsuitable and in them they are incongruous and out of place. It is perfectly true, that being sinners we are not worthy either to offer praise or to join in the offering of the Perpetual Memory which Christ ordained, and need to ask for grace to cleanse and fit us for those acts. But the Invitation says nought of fitness for praise, but of the requisites for receiving the Sacrament. And the "intention" of the Confession, Absolution and Comfortable Words is determined by this Invitation by which they are prefaced. Referring to Reception, they are out of place before the Eucharistic Act. There was indeed an Inclination or other prayer acknowledging unworthiness and seeking Divine Grace before the Eucharistic Act or at the Offertory, in many or most Eastern Liturgies, but this referred to the Offering of the Memorial and Offering which Christ appointed and not to Reception.

The "*Prayer of Humble Access*," again, refers exclusively to reception and not to joining in the Offering made in the Consecration Prayer. Coming, as it does, before the Consecration, it is quite out of place. The incongruity is made somewhat less apparent, at the present time, by the near proximity of the Reception. But with the desirable restoration of the Invocation, Oblation and Intercession after the Consecration Prayer, the interval would be increased and the incorrectness of its place more clearly seen and felt.

Then there is the void before Reception. There

is—contrary to every example—no solemn devotion of penitence and humility before Reception. No liturgical provision is made. The Communicants are left to their own thoughts or to help provided in unofficial manuals. And finally the present arrangement interrupts the due sequence of ideas. Instead of the Godward part being rendered and completed first, before the manward part is entered upon, there is (as it were) a constant see-saw. First the attention is turned to GOD in the prayer for the Church, then down to ourselves in the Invitation, etc.; then back to GOD in the Eucharistic Act (Sursum, etc.); then again to ourselves in the Prayer of Humble Access; once again to GOD in the Consecration Prayer and back to ourselves again in the Communion.

The fitness of things, the due sequence of ideas, and ancient precedent demand a restoration of the Communicants' Preparation (viz. the Lord's Prayer and Embolismus, the Invitation, Confession, Absolution, Comfortable Words and Prayer of Humble Access) to the true position, immediately before the Communion. Then the worshippers could render to GOD His due and play their part as priests unto GOD with undivided thoughts, and, that done, turn to prepare to receive the GIFT.

CHAPTER XII

ABSENCE OF EXPLICIT PRAYER FOR THE DEPARTED IN THE INTERCESSION

EXAMINATION of the Intercession in the Primitive Liturgies shows that in every case the Intercession included not only many and various conditions of the living, but also the departed members of the Church.

S. Cyril of Jerusalem says: "Then we make mention of all that have fallen asleep before us, first for Patriarchs, Prophets, Apostles, Martyrs, that GOD would receive our supplication for their prayers and intercessions; then also for the holy fathers and bishops who have fallen asleep and all in fact who among us have fallen asleep." (Brightman, *Liturgies Eastern and Western*, Vol. I. p. 466.)

Then we turn to the Liturgies. From these we will give illustrations of their treatment of this matter.

The *Clementine* (Brightman, *op. cit.* p. 21) in the *Intercession* has, "Moreover we offer unto Thee also for all who have from the beginning pleased Thee, the holy patriarchs, prophets, righteous men, apostles, martyrs... and all whose names Thou knowest."

And in the *Inclination* following:

"Let us pray for those who have entered into their rest in the faith" (*ibid.* p. 23).

Bishop Serapion's Intercession: "We intercede also on behalf of all who have been laid to rest, whose memorial we are making. [After the recitation of the names] "Sanctify these souls: for Thou knowest all. Sanctify all (souls) laid to rest in the Lord. And number them with all Thy holy powers and give to them a place and a mansion in Thy Kingdom." (Ed. Wordsworth, S.P.C.K. p. 64.)

S. James (Brightman, *op. cit.* p. 56 and sq.): "Further vouchsafe to remember those who have pleased Thee from the beginning, generation by generation, the holy fathers, patriarchs, prophets, apostles, martyrs, confessors, teachers, saints and every just soul made perfect in the faith of Thy Christ....Not that we are worthy to mention their blessedness, but that they even standing beside Thy fearful and terrible throne may in turn recall our misery and that we may find grace and pity before Thee, O Lord, to our timely aid.

"Remember, O Lord, the GOD of the spirits and of all flesh, those whom we commemorate and those whom we do not commemorate, of the Orthodox, from Abel the Just to the present day: Thyself give them rest in the land of the living, in Thy Kingdom, in the delight of Paradise, in the bosom of Abraham, Isaac and Jacob, our holy fathers, whence pain, sorrow, and groaning is exiled, where the light of Thy countenance looks down and always shines. And direct the end of our lives... gathering us under the feet of Thine elect...."

The Syrian Jacobite (Brightman, *op. cit.* p. 92 and sq.): " Remember all who have been well pleasing to Thee since the world began...Remember also...holy Bishops...by whose prayers and supplications grant Thy peace to Thy Church.   Their doctrines and their confession confirm in our souls...remember those whom we have mentioned...Rest their souls and bodies and spirits, deliver them from eternal punishment to come, and vouchsafe to them delight in the bosom....Impute to them none of their offences...."

S. Mark (Brightman, *op. cit.* p. 128 and sq.): " Rest the souls of our fathers and brethren who have fallen asleep....Rest their souls and vouchsafe to them the kingdom of heaven ; and to us grant...a portion and a lot with all Thy Saints."

The Nestorian (Brightman, *op. cit.* p. 275 and sq.): " Let us pray and beseech GOD the Lord of all, that this oblation be accepted for all the just and righteous fathers who were well pleasing in His sight....And for all them that in a true faith departed from this world of whom our Lord alone knoweth the names, that Elohim crown them in the resurrection of the dead."

S. Basil (Brightman, *op. cit.* p. 330 and sq.): " That Thou wouldest unite all of us in the fellowship of one Holy Spirit and not cause any of us to partake of the holy Body and Blood of Christ to judgement but that we may find mercy and grace with all Thy Saints...."

The Armenian (Brightman, *op. cit.* p. 440): "Through this give rest to all those who aforetime have fallen asleep in Christ, to our forefathers...who have died in the faith, with whom we also beseech Thee, good GOD, to visit us."

The Mozarabic: "Item offerunt universi Presbyteri, Diaconi, Clerici ac Populi circumadstantes in honorem Sanctorum pro se et suis." [Chorus: "Offerunt pro se et pro universâ fraternitate."]

"Facientes commemorationem Beatissimorum Apostolorum, etc....Item pro spiritibus pausantium...vivant in nobis, Jesu Domine, Apostoli tui Jacobi praedicamenta doctrinae...quo...in pace et charitate nunc et in aeternum tecum sine fine vivamus....

"Suscipe, Jesu bone, in hoc natali Jacobi Apostoli tui offerentium vota, et refrigerium praesta spiritibus defunctorum; ut, eo apud Te intercedente, et viventibus et defunctis tuae pietatis gratia impendatur...." (*Missae Goth. et Officii Muzarabici Expositio*, Lorenzana, pp. 36 and 37.)

Gallican: "Placate, Domine, quaesumus, humilitatis nostrae precibus et hostiis...et eorum nomina qui nos praecesserunt cum signo fidei, et dormiunt in somno pacis, ipsis et omnibus in Christo quiescentibus locum refrigerii, lucis et pacis ut indulgeas, deprecamur." Mabillon, *De Lit. Gallic.* p. 333 (Advent Mass).

Roman. Before Consecration: "Communicantes et memoriam venerantes in primis...et omnium sanctorum tuorum: quorum meritis precibusque concedas, ut in omnibus protectionis tuae muniamur auxilio."

After Consecration: "Memento etiam, Domine, famulorum famularumque tuarum (N. et N.) qui nos praecesserunt cum signo fidei et dormiunt in somno pacis. Ipsis, Domine, et omnibus in Christo quiescentibus locum refrigerii, lucis et pacis, ut indulgeas, deprecamur.

"Nobis quoque...partem aliquem et societatem donare digneris cum tuis sanctis...."

Reviewing the whole, we see that there came[1] to be a general distinction between the Saints of note and the ordinary faithful departed. The former are commemorated and for them thanks is given; and the benefit of their intercession is requested and the recollection and following of their teaching and example by the living is besought. The latter are prayed for that they may receive pardon, peace and bliss. And to this twofold supplication for others departed, is very generally added a petition for the worshippers for a share with them in the resurrection to life and eternal bliss.

Now in the First Book of Edward VI. this general treatment is followed.

"And here we do give unto Thee most high praise and hearty thanks for the wonderful grace and virtue declared in all Thy Saints from the beginning of the world, and chiefly in the glorious and most blessed Virgin Mary, Mother of Thy Son Jesus Christ, our Lord and GOD, and in the holy Patriarchs, Prophets, Apostles, and Martyrs, whose examples (O Lord) and stedfastness in Thy Faith and keeping Thy holy Commandments grant us to follow. We commend unto Thy mercy,

---

[1] Originally in all probability this did not exist. For, in the Clementine and the Book of Bishop Serapion, for example, intercession seems to be made for all.

O Lord, all other Thy servants, which are departed hence from us, with the sign of faith[1] and now do rest in the sleep of peace: grant unto them, we beseech Thee, Thy mercy and everlasting peace[2] and that at the day of the General Resurrection, we and all they which be of the mystical body of Thy Son, may altogether be set at His right hand and hear that His most joyful voice, 'Come unto Me, O ye that be blessed of My Father, and possess the Kingdom which is prepared for you from the beginning of the world.' Grant this, O Father," etc.

When we turn to *our Office*, what we have is: "And we also bless Thy holy name for all Thy servants departed this life in Thy faith and fear, beseeching Thee to give us grace to follow their good examples, that with them we may be partakers of Thy heavenly kingdom."

Here is thanksgiving for the lives of holy men, but there is no direct and explicit *prayer* for any but ourselves, the living, that " we may follow their good examples" and "be partakers of Thy heavenly kingdom." This thanksgiving and this prayer are after general precedent. But there is no distinction made in the thanksgiving between the Saints of special note and the ordinary devout Christian departed. This fails to recognise the imperfections of the ordinary men and women on their departure albeit " in the faith and fear of GOD." There also is no plain petition for them, for their sanctification, rest and peace as in older models.

---

[1] Quotation from the Roman.   [2] Recalls the Gallican.

But there are the words "with them" prefixed to the request that we may "be partakers of Thy heavenly kingdom." "*With them*" may mean that they are already partakers of the heavenly kingdom, and that we pray to join them. This interpretation would be without precedent in Catholic Theology. For, while it has not uncommonly been held that the Apostles and Martyrs already have been admitted to the Beatific Vision, it has never been advanced, except by modern Protestantism, that *all* the godly departed—who are alone here mentioned—attain at death to heaven, which can be the only sense of the heavenly kingdom.

The alternative meaning of "with them" is, a petition that "they as well as ourselves may *at last* attain to the heavenly kingdom."

So taken, the whole forms, as it were, a compressed quotation from S. Mark: "Rest their souls and vouchsafe to them the kingdom of heaven: and to us grant... a portion and a lot with all Thy Saints."

The passage was only introduced in 1662 and was no doubt modelled on the prayer already in the Burial Service: "accomplish the number of Thy elect...that we with all those that are departed in the true faith of Thy holy name, may have our perfect consummation and bliss...in Thy eternal and everlasting glory": and also on the phrase in the Book of 1549 and the Scottish Office of 1637: "that we and all they which be of the mystical body of Thy Son may altogether be set at His right hand and hear...voice...come, possess the Kingdom...." Here obviously "we and all they altogether" is a prayer that they, as well as we, may, at the future Judgement, enter into the Kingdom.

Wheatley, therefore, said long ago, "though the direct petition for the faithful departed is still discontinued, yet, were it not for the restriction of the words '*militant here on earth*,' they might be supposed to be implied in our present form, when we beg of GOD, that we with them may be partakers of His heavenly kingdom." *Rational Illustration B.C.P.* p. 279. To many still, these words seem to preclude this inclusion.

But it may be pointed out that the same title ("a general and devout prayer for the good state of our mother the Church, militant here in earth") was borne by a prayer[1] in a book of "Hours" of 1531, which included at the end a definite prayer for the departed, viz. "and to all the faithful living and departed, grant eternal life and kingdom together (pariter) in the land of the living."

In the Scottish book of 1637 which had the main substance of the prayer for the departed from the Book of 1549, the same title was at the head. In that book of 1637 the prayer for the departed under this title was, "And we also bless Thy holy name for all Thy Servants, who having finished their course in faith, do now rest from their labours. And we do yield unto

---

[1] The prayer is printed in *Directorium Anglicanum*, p. 68, 3rd edition, 1866. The book was "Horae Beatae Mariae Virginis ad usum ecclesiae Sarum ex officina Christophori Ruremunden 1531." The book was then, 1866, in a private collection.

Thee most high praise," etc. [as in 1549 as far as] "to saints, who have been the choice vessels of Thy grace and lights of the world in their several generations; most humbly beseeching Thee, that we may have grace to follow the example of their stedfastness in Thy faith and obedience to Thy Commandments, that at the day of the general resurrection, we and all they which be of the mystical body of Thy Son, may altogether be set on His right hand," etc.

In the revision of 1661, when reference to the departed was restored in our amended form, it was sought to change the designation. In the book presented to the commissioners with the proposed change, we find a fresh title, written and erased, "Let us pray for the good estate of the Catholic Church of Christ." This indicates the intention of the revisers, and the meaning which they attached to the sentence, which they had appended to the prayer. They meant by "with them," to pray for the entrance of those in the Church *at rest*, as well as that of the living, into the heavenly kingdom.

Their abandonment of the new title indicates merely their desire to placate opposition, and their content to follow Laud's precedent of 1637 in using a title not fully comprehending the contents of the prayer and yet by ancient example not excluding prayer for the departed.

The conclusion therefore seems reasonable and almost certain, that the words "with them" involve an implicit prayer for the faithful departed.

The contrary view, excluding all reference to the departed, would not invalidate the rite, but it would be a departure from universal practice from the earliest days, and it would maim the fulness of the Intercession.

As it is, on the above assumption, we have but to lament the absence of explicit and plain terms, such as the uninstructed might recognise instead of this covert allusion.

Such covert allusion is a defect. The sense of public prayers should be simple and obvious.

There is a further defect in absence of distinction between those who have led lives of special sanctity or done special service, and those who have led lives of ordinary or even of indifferent character. And besides, this prayer refers only to the Last Day (if we construe as we have done, as a prayer for the departed) and says nothing of the present. The departed and especially the greater and latter class need our prayers now. The general manner was to supplicate—at first for all, and later, excluding the special saints—for the rest and peace and perfecting of the departed now.

Though the prayer that they may be partakers of the everlasting kingdom, no doubt implies all this, it ought to be expressed.

Of the cognate rites, the Scottish retained the form of 1637 quoted above, but omitted the title. The Non-jurors' Office likewise omitted the title, but adopted the exact wording of Edward's First Book. The American form has the same wording as ours but omits "on earth" from the title.

CHAPTER XIII

VERBAL OBLATION OF THE ELEMENTS

In reflecting on the Institution of the Sacrament, and the considerations involved, it appeared desirable that there should be a petition asking acceptance of the material Elements.

Accordingly we find such a petition in practically all the Liturgies.

The Elements are brought and placed on the Altar, and a prayer is offered in which, in some terms or other, their acceptance is besought.

For example in the *Greek S. James*, we find the direction, "The Priest bringing in the holy gifts says this prayer: O God...Thyself bless this Offering and receive it at Thy heavenly altar." Brightman, *Liturgies Eastern and Western*, Vol. I. p. 41.

The Sarum had: "Receive, O Holy Trinity, this oblation..." after the Priest had received and placed the Elements on the Altar.

When we turn to our own Office we find no form of words provided specifically for this purpose. And there are no words capable of being referred to any verbal offering of the Elements, except those at the beginning of the Prayer for the Church militant: viz.

"we humbly beseech Thee to accept our alms and oblations." And the historical meaning of this phrase is open to considerable difference of opinion.

The words "and oblations" were only inserted in 1662. In the first and following English Prayer Books they were absent. At the same time as these words were introduced, a new rubric was composed and placed after that concerning the collection, and just before this prayer. This orders "the placing" of Bread and Wine upon the Table and is a version of a rubric inserted in the Scottish Office of 1637, which spoke of "offering" the Bread and Wine.

As a commentary, we read in Bishop Patrick's *Mensa Mystica*, "We pray Him therefore, in our Communion Service, to accept our oblations (meaning those of bread and wine) as well as our alms." These words are absent from the first edition of 1660, before the insertion of these words in the prayer, but are found in the edition of 1667 and subsequent editions, after their insertion. From these facts, it might be reasonably concluded that "oblations" refers to the "elements," and that here we have in fact a verbal offering of the Elements to God for His acceptance after the common primitive manner.

And we have expressions of several learned divines of that age to support this interpretation of the word of the Elements. To quote two only. Dean Field (*Of the Church*, 1621), "oblation of the people is meant that consisteth of bread and wine, brought and set upon the Lord's Table."

Thorndike in 1659: "The Elements of the Eucharist before they be consecrated are truly accounted *oblations* or sacrifices."

And Wheatley, writing later, on this rubric and the general principle, says, "Which rubric being added to our Liturgy at the same time with the word 'oblations,' in the prayer following...it is clearly evident...that by that word are to be understood the elements of bread and wine, which the priest is to offer solemnly to GOD, as an acknowledgement of His sovereignty over His creatures and that from henceforth they might become properly and peculiarly His." *Rational Illustration of B.C.P.* p. 271.

But against this, Bishop Dowden (*Further Studies in P.B.* p. 176) sets the rejection of the words "offer up" in the rubric ordering the placing of the Elements on the Altar.

Next, he calls attention to the Scottish rubric of 1637 concerning the Collection, in which the Collector is to "reverently bring the said bason with the oblations therein and deliver it to the Presbyter."

Many instances of the use of oblations for money offerings other than gifts to the poor (alms) are found in Ancient Synodals, and in the Royal Injunctions of 1547. And Bishop Andrewes in the form of Consecration of Jesus Chapel, Southampton, in 1620 introduced a prayer for "all who come into this Thy Holy Temple, when they offer, that their *oblation and alms* may come up," etc.

And an inventory shows that in his own chapel he had two basons, one for "offerings" and one for "alms."

And a rubric in the service for the Consecration of Christ Church, Tynemouth, 1668, by Bishop Cosin, directs the Bishop to offer his own "alms and oblations": "Then one of the priests shall receive the *alms and oblations*[1]."

And Dean Comber's *Companion to the Temple* (1675) has a paraphrase of the prayer for the whole Church, in which we read, " our alms to the poor and *oblations to Thy ministers*, intreating," etc. And in the margin he has the note, "This is to be omitted when there is no collection."

To endeavour to sum up :

It seems clear that at the time of its insertion into this prayer, Oblation was used in two recognised senses—of the Elements and of money offerings to objects other than to the poor, and specially for the maintenance of the clergy.

We have illustrations from a sister rite, and from special services drawn up by Bishops Andrewes and Cosin, of the use in conjunction with alms, of " oblation " for a money offering. Of the two contemporary commentators, Patrick and Comber, one explains in one sense and one in the other.

There is no doubt it was doubly understood from the first. The question is what did the revisers mean ? The use of Cosin and Sancroft might seem to point to the interpretation as money offerings (other than offer-

---

[1] Sancroft, who was Chaplain to Cosin and acted as Clerk to the revision Convocation, asked at his visitation in 1686, "are the alms and oblations of devout persons duly collected and received ?"

ings to the poor) as the mind of the revisers. Yet Cosin was only one (and Sancroft is dependent on him). May not the truth be that Convocation, which put in the word, was divided in its intention and interpretation ? Is it not another instance of " comprehension "— using a phrase patient of diverse interpretation, to meet the views of two parties ?

The application of the word to the Elements is, we venture to think, perfectly valid, as one of two possible interpretations.

If then the word " oblations " does stand for the bread and wine, we have what the considerations of completeness and fitness desiderate.

But if not, and in consequence, the Office is without a verbal form asking acceptance for the Bread and Wine, there is nothing in this to make our Office insufficient, or even peculiar.

In the " Clementine " Liturgy and the Early Roman Ordo there is nothing but the rubric directing the placing of the Elements on the Altar.

While in the Syrian Jacobite, the Coptic, and Abyssinian there is no prayer at the placing of the Elements on the Altar (though prayers of this kind occurred in the preparation of the Elements prior to the Office).

At the same time words to accompany the solemn placing of the Elements on the Altar are highly desirable.

CHAPTER XIV

GENERAL CONCLUSIONS

IN gathering up our conclusions, I venture to think that any charge of insufficiency in our Office may be taken as disproved. There may be an eccentricity of order, there may be a dislocation of structure, there may be in certain particulars poverty of expression, but the essentials are there. To interpolate portions of the old Sarum Canon before and after the Consecration prayer is unnecessary and it involves vain repetition, if not absurdity, because our Office is but a re-editing of the Office of 1549: and the Office of 1549 was but a translation and revision of the old Sarum Canon. In the Appendix will be found a harmony or synopsis, in which will be seen the close way (on the whole) in which the revisers of 1549 followed the structure of the Sarum Canon: and the large degree of verbal identity between that Office and theirs of 1549. To interpolate from the Sarum Canon its intercession and oblation into our Office, is to say the same prayers over twice, in two versions. At the same time our Office has grave defects which call for remedy.

I. First and chiefly there is a grievous confusion and disorder of structure.

a. There is a *separation between the Consecration Prayer* (i.e. the Commemoration of Redemption and the Narrative of Institution) and

    (i)   the Eucharistic Act;

    (ii)   the Prayer of Oblation;

    (iii) the Intercession.

β. The Invocation, as far as our Office has one, is in the middle of our Consecration Prayer ("Hear us, etc....Blood"), before the Narrative of the Institution, instead of in the course of the Prayer of Oblation.

Now by the 4th century, the Eastern and Gallican structure was such, that the Offertory was followed by the Eucharistic Act, the Consecration, Invocation and Oblation, and then the Intercession.

Our Office needs rearranging, so that

(1) The "Eucharistic Act" (from the "Sursum Corda" to the end of the "Sanctus") follows upon the Offertory, when the Elements are presented and placed on the Altar;

(2) Then immediately after the Sanctus should come the Consecration Prayer (without the clause of Invocation);

(3) And following on that, the Prayer of Oblation[1] (with the Invocation embodied);

(4) And after that the "Prayer for the whole Church."

This gives a structure not only after the very

[1] As to the composition of that prayer, we shall speak below.

general and early model, but which is rational and simple.

Having brought the Gifts which Christ commanded,

(1) We offer thanks and praise to GOD for all His Mercy and lastly for sending His Son;

(2) Then we allege Christ's Command to us to continue this Memorial, we narrate what He did at His Institution and imitate Him;

(3) We ask Him to accept our service, and to send down His Spirit to make these creatures means of grace: we ask that through this service we and the whole Church may receive the benefits of the Passion.

(4) And then we proceed to the Intercession, wherein we bring definite objects forward that they may receive those benefits.

γ. The Preparation of the Communicant is split up and comes in part before and part after the Eucharistic Act, quite away from the actual time of Communion.

In the 4th century at Jerusalem, the Lord's Prayer was said and the Elevation[1] with the solemn reminder " Holy things for Holy people." The Eastern Liturgies also had a " prayer of Inclination " or " Humble Access " and a Blessing.

All this always immediately before the time of Reception.

In our Office, therefore, the Lord's Prayer should be shorn of its Doxology and restored to its original place, before the Communion. Likewise the place of

---

[1] This has its equivalent in our "Invitation "—see Appendix.

the Invitation, Confession, Absolution, Comfortable Words and Prayer of Humble Access should again be before the Communion.

Our Office would then run:

The Offertory.

The Eucharistic Act ["Sursum Corda" to the end of the "Sanctus"].

The Consecration Prayer.

The Prayer of Oblation (containing the Invocation).

The Intercession [the Prayer for the whole Church].

The Lord's Prayer.

The Invitation, Confession, Absolution, Comfortable Words and Prayer of Humble Access.

The Communion.

The Prayer of Thanksgiving ("Almighty and Ever-living GOD," etc.) and Gloria.

The Blessing.

In this restoration and amendment, the Scottish Liturgy of 1761 has shown us the way.

But the subsequent American Office adopts only the single reform (in this matter of structure), of placing the Prayer of Oblation (containing the Invocation after the old manner) after the Prayer of Consecration. This redresses the most serious blemish in our Office, which severs the prayer for acceptance of our Memorial from narrative of its Institution. But it still leaves the interruption between the Eucharistic Act and the Prayer of Consecration.

The barest minimum of reform must include (besides what the American Liturgy has done) the removal of the Prayer of Humble Access and the placing of it immediately before Reception.

This would remove the gravest defects of order and structure. But the full rearrangement is the true object of prayer and effort.

Then we should have an Office after the model of the East in the 4th century or earlier, and one of the most beautiful and marked with a straightforward simplicity and terseness, such as the genius of our race demands.

II. There are also defects in form.

There is need of

a. Thanksgiving for the mercies of the Incarnation and Redemption, in place of the mere reference (by the way, so to speak) to the Redemption on the Cross in opening the Consecration Prayer;

β. An explicit Invocation;

γ. A fuller form of Oblation;

δ. A more definite prayer for the Departed;

ε. A more definite oblation of the Elements.

(*a*) The "*Prayer of Consecration*" opens with a mere acknowledgement of the Blessing of Redemption instead of with Thanksgiving for it as in the Eastern and Gothic models.

The Scottish Office and its offspring the American show the way in quite a simple manner, viz. "All glory be to Thee, Almighty GOD, our heavenly Father, for that Thou of Thy tender mercy didst give Thy only Son," etc., as in our Office.

Here is definite offering of adoration and praise,

with the slightest alteration of our form. Surely it is not too much to hope, that this might be adopted in our Office.

The Nonjurors' Office of 1718 provides a richer form on the lines of the "Clementine" form and that of S. James. But the Scottish form is more suitable to the reserve of our temperament, as well as admitting the retention of our familiar phrasing.

(β)   *The Invocation.*

The nature of the case and universal precedent demand some supplication for the intervention of Divine Power to fit the natural elements for their use as means of the Grace of the Sacrament.

In our Office we ask, " Hear us...and grant that we receiving these Thy creatures of Bread and Wine, according...may be partakers of His most precious BODY and BLOOD."

And this comes in the course of the Prayer of Consecration, instead of in the course of the Prayer of Oblation following. To this latter place it needs removing and its form making more explicit. There should be a direct request for the intervention of Divine Power to make the symbols efficacious signs, and means whereby we receive the BODY and BLOOD of Christ. " Hear us, we beseech Thee, most merciful Father, and vouchsafe to hallow and bless these Thy creatures of bread and wine that we receiving them according to Thy Son's Holy Institution, in remembrance of His death and passion, may be partakers," etc.

But reform should go further. Christendom had

come in the 4th century to see that the Holy Ghost is the agent of Divine hallowing and giving of life. We should do well to follow the Eastern method, universal from the 4th century, and make a direct request for the coming of the Holy Spirit upon the Elements to hallow them and add grace to them, making them valid for the conveyance of the Grace of the Sacrament.

Both the Scottish form of 1761 and the American Liturgies suggest examples. The Scottish form is:

"And we most humbly beseech Thee, O merciful Father, to hear us and of Thy Almighty goodness vouchsafe to bless and sanctify with Thy Word and Holy Spirit, these Thy gifts and creatures of Bread and Wine, that they may become the BODY and BLOOD of Thy most dearly beloved Son. And we most earnestly desire Thy Fatherly goodness," etc., as in our Prayer of Oblation.

This form has the merit of definiteness as to the objective reality of the Sacramental Gift. But it is brief to baldness. The phrase in the Latin Canon and the early book of Serapion was, "become unto us." This would satisfy the needs of the case. But the Revised Text, recently authorised by the Scottish Synod, runs: "And humbly praying that it may be unto us according to His Word, we Thine unworthy servants beseech Thee, most merciful Father, to hear us and to send Thy Holy Spirit upon us and upon these Thy gifts and creatures of Bread and Wine, that being blessed and hallowed by His lifegiving power they may become the BODY and BLOOD of Thy most dearly beloved Son, to the end that whosoever shall receive the same, may be sanctified both in body and soul and preserved unto everlasting life."

This is a great enrichment. But the sentence "humbly praying...word" seems to make for unnecessary diffuseness.

The addition "upon us" is after the example of S. James and other old Eastern Liturgies and is not inappropriate where (as here) to the petition for the gift of the "Res Sacramenti," is added a petition for the reception of the "Virtus Sacramenti."

The *American* is a combination of the form of 1549 and that of our Office. "We most humbly beseech Thee, O merciful Father, to hear us, and of Thy Almighty goodness, vouchsafe to bless and sanctify with Thy Word and Holy Spirit these Thy creatures of Bread and Wine": from the Book of 1549, and then from our book, "that we receiving...may be partakers," etc. This remedies the chief defect of our book in that it directly solicits the action of the Spirit's power. But it labours under the same defect as our form in the lack of definite reference to the "Res Sacramenti" as the object of that action of the Spirit, as apart from the "Virtus Sacramenti," though in this, it has the precedent of the forms in the Nestorian Liturgy and the Liturgy of Malabar.

The revised form of the Scottish Office would be a beautiful enrichment of our Office, though in any revision, the American form might more easily obtain acceptance, because of its affinity with the phrasing of the form to which we are accustomed. But in the event of its adoption, it would seem desirable that the words "Thy Word and" before "Holy Spirit," should be omitted. Because if by "Thy Word" the Divine Logos is intended, there would seem to be redundancy in the invocation of both the Second and Third Persons of the Trinity. While, if as has been argued in the chapter on this subject, "word" in 1549 meant "formula," i.e. the Narrative of Institution, it would be an anachronism after the formula had been said.

(γ) *The Form of Oblation.*

Our Office only asks GOD "mercifully to accept this our Sacrifice of Praise and Thanksgiving." This is quite sufficient designation of the service according to ancient precedent, and sufficient pleading of the Memorial. At the same time, the fitness of things would suggest some specification of the various details of Christ's work of Redemption: and devotion surely demands a full recounting of the various acts of redeeming love.

The older Liturgies are unanimous in making mention of His Resurrection and Glorious Ascension as well as the Passion; and most also plead His Session in Heaven and Second Coming.

The Scottish and American agree with the Book of 1549: "Wherefore, O Lord, and heavenly Father, according to the Institution of Thy dearly beloved Son, our Saviour Jesus Christ, we Thy humble servants do celebrate and make here before Thy Divine Majesty with these Thy holy Gifts, which we now offer unto Thee, the Memorial Thy Son hath commanded us to make; having in remembrance His blessed Passion and precious Death, His mighty Resurrection and glorious Ascension; rendering unto Thee most hearty thanks for the innumerable benefits procured unto us by the same, and looking for His coming again with power and great glory." [The Book of 1549 and the American do not include the last sentence "and looking," etc., which so much enriches the form.]

Then would follow the Invocation and after that our prayer of Oblation—except that the sentence " we who are partakers of this Holy Communion" needs restoring to its form of 1549, "we who shall be partakers of this Holy Communion, may worthily receive the most precious BODY and BLOOD of Thy Son Jesus Christ and be fulfilled with Thy Grace," etc.

(δ) *Prayer for the Departed.*

This is a universal feature of the Intercession.

There was generally a thanksgiving for the Saints and prayer for all departed in the fear of GOD.

In our Office we bless GOD "for all departed in Thy faith and fear, beseeching Thee to give us grace so to follow their good examples, that with them we may be partakers of Thy Heavenly Kingdom." Here the only prayer that is *obvious* is for *ourselves*: viz. "that we may follow their examples" and enter into the Heavenly Kingdom.

Although "with them" implies the petition for their entrance (we have seen) as well as ours.

What is wanted is:

(i) *The Commemoration of the Saints.*

There used to be mention of names, and a thanksgiving for illustrious examples as in the Scottish Office would be very desirable: "we yield unto Thee most high praise and hearty thanks, for the wonderful grace and virtue declared in all Thy Saints, who have been the chosen vessels of Thy grace, and the lights of the world in their several generations." Then would come the mention of the godly departed in general, "And we bless Thy Holy Name for all Thy servants departed this life in Thy faith and fear." Of course this latter does include the former: but separate mention would enable us to more readily include the thought of our own departed, at the time of the prayer's use.

(ii) *The prayer to follow their good example.* "Beseeching Thee to give us grace to follow their good examples," or shortly, "Whose examples grant us to follow."

(iii) *Prayer for the Departed.*

This might be quite simple as in the Armenian. "To all those who have fallen asleep in Christ give rest." Or more fully than "give rest," the form of 1549 might be followed, "grant Thy mercy and everlasting peace."

Or, to take an uncommon line, we might adopt Bishop Serapion's intercession, "Sanctify all laid to rest in the Lord."

(iv) *Prayer for the final union of all in Christ.* "And grant that at the general day of Resurrection, we, and all they who are of the mystical Body of Thy Son, may be set at His right hand, and hear His most joyful voice, " Come, ye blessed of My Father, inherit the kingdom prepared for you from the foundation of the world ": as the Scottish and English of 1549.

The whole would then run:

" And we yield unto Thee most [high praise and] hearty thanks, for the wonderful grace and virtue declared in all Thy Saints, who have been the chosen vessels of Thy grace, and the lights of the world in their several generations;

" And we bless Thy holy name for *all* Thy servants departed this life in Thy faith and fear;

" Whose examples grant us to follow;

" And to all those who have fallen asleep in Christ give sanctification, mercy and everlasting peace;

" And grant that at the day of the general Resurrection," etc.

(ε) *More definite Oblation of the Elements.*

Considerations of fitness led to the very general use of a prayer for the acceptance of the natural elements.

In our Office there is nothing but the possible reference in the word "oblations," in the opening of the Prayer for the Church Militant. So long as this prayer immediately follows the placing of the Bread and Wine on the Altar this may be taken to serve, though it is not explicit, while if (as is to be hoped) the Intercession were moved into connection with the Greater Oblation the want of a form to accompany this Lesser Oblation would be badly felt.

There is a form to hand in the Coronation Service quite after the ancient manner. The Archbishop " reverently places [the bread and wine] on the altar... first saying,

" ' Bless, O Lord...these Thy gifts and sanctify them to this holy use, that by them we may be made partakers of the BODY and BLOOD of Thy only begotten Son Jesus Christ and fed unto everlasting life of soul and body.' "

In the Scottish Office there is also a form. This is after the rubric " And the presbyter shall then offer up and place the bread and wine prepared for the Sacrament, upon the Lord's table and shall say :

" ' Blessed be Thou, O Lord God, for ever and ever. Thine, O Lord, is the greatness and the glory and the victory and the majesty : for all that is in the heaven and in the earth is Thine : Thine is the Kingdom, O Lord, and Thou art exalted as head above all ; both riches and honour come of Thee, and of Thine own do we give unto Thee.' " This is very grand, but the former is simpler and more explicit. On that account, if one or the other had to be chosen, the former is preferable. It would make a noble feature of the Office to use both, the Scottish first and then that from the Coronation Office, as far as transcribed.

III. It will be seen that the desire of the writer is to adopt the lines of the Scottish Service. In our Office the main prominence is given to Communion. Coming as it does in the midst of the Office, it makes the Form of Oblation and what follows a mere appendix. The memorial side of the Office is quite obscured to the ordinary reader and user of the Office. No doubt there was excuse for reforming zeal in the 16th century, in the general neglect of Communion, along with general attendance at the Service to join in the Memorial. But the pendulum has swung the other way thanks to the exaggeration of 1552. Notwithstanding the prominence given in the Catechism, the Memorial side is largely and widely unrealised now. What is required is clear expression of both sides—the Memorial and Sacramental sides—of the Rite to the exclusion or depression of neither. There ought not to be disinclination to acknowledge past mistakes. There ought not to be fear of expressing a truth, for fear of exaggeration or abuse.

The reform of our Office desired in these pages would simply, in a calmer age than the 16th century, provide for a fuller and more distinct treatment of the twofold purpose of the Eucharist, "for the continual remembrance of the Sacrifice of the Death of Christ" and "for the strengthening and refreshing of our souls."

The gathering together of the Eucharistic Act, Narrative of Institution, Oblation, Invocation and Intercession, would give distinct prominence to the Memorial.

The gathering together again of the sundered parts of the Communicants' Preparation and placing of them before the Act of Communion, would give a solemnity and prominence to Communion which could not be overlooked. In a word the Office would then appear to all and casual beholders as it truly is, a mountain with two sublime peaks reaching to heaven, a pleading of Christ's work and an approach in Communion: instead of as a mountain of one peak only—Communion.

In conclusion, the opinions of two writers widely separated, may be quoted.

Writing to Rev. J. Skinner[1] in 1806, Bishop Horsley says, "With respect to the comparative merit of the two Offices of England and Scotland, I have no scruple in declaring...that I think the Scotch Office more conformable to the primitive models, and in my private judgement more edifying than that which we now use...nevertheless I think our present Office is very good, and our form of Consecration of the Elements is sufficient; I mean that the Elements are consecrated by it and made the Body and Blood of Christ in the sense in which our Lord Himself said the bread and wine were His Body and Blood."

And Bishop Thirlwall, an able scholar of judicious and detached temper (Charge 1857, republished in *Remains Literary and Theological*, I. 279), writes: "There are passages in the Scottish Office, which, as it appears to me, add much to its solemnity, without being liable to any misconception in point of doctrine. They express that which in the English Office is *tacitly implied*, but is left to be understood and therefore *may easily be overlooked*. But the main difference between the two Offices consists in the greater prominence which is

---

[1] Quoted in Bishop Dowden's *Annotated Scotch Communion Office*, p. 106.

given in the Scottish Office to the commemorative
character of the rite....It is clear that in the view of
the framers of this Liturgy, the interval between
Consecration and Communion is the most appropriate
season for all manner of supplications, general and
special, which are founded on the great sacrifice commemorated in the Eucharist. I must own that I do
not see any valid doctrinal objection to this view,
though I am aware that it may be carried out in a
manner liable to great abuse."

Thankful we must be for the Providence which
preserved our Office from insufficiency in what is
essential for the Consecration of the Sacrament and
for the making of the Memorial.

Thankful we must be for the simple grandeur and
music of its phrasing, hallowed and made dear to us by
long use and association.

But thankfulness may not blind us to defects that
might easily be remedied and which have been
remedied in our sister Church of Scotland and (partly)
in our daughter Church of the United States.

With the remedy of these, we should indeed have
a Liturgy which would occupy a position unique in the
world of Liturgies, for beauty of diction, simplicity
of treatment, straightforwardness of structure and completeness of composition.

The lovers of Zion should direct their prayers and
efforts, that the Lord, whom we desire to worship more
perfectly, may hasten in His time the fulfilment of
these aims.

APPENDIX A

THE MANUAL ACTS

THE Sacred Record not only speaks of blessing and thanksgiving by our Lord at the Institution; He also " brake " the Bread for distribution among the Disciples. The Liturgies of SS. James and Basil and the Liturgy of the Syrian Jacobites also perpetuate the tradition of an Elevation. " He took the Bread and showed it (ἀναδείξας) to His Father." (Brightman, *Liturgies Eastern and Western,* Vol. I. pp. 52, 327 and 87.)

Accordingly in the Eucharistic ceremonial there came to be an imitation of these actions, although not at the same time or with the same intent. They may be conveniently classed as the Manual Acts. In the Byzantine Rite and in S. James and S. Mark they followed the Lord's Prayer. In other rites they were partly before and partly after it.

I. *The Elevation.*

Though the tradition was preserved of our Lord's elevation of the Elements at the Institution, no actual elevation by the celebrant was ordered or used in the Eastern Liturgies at the recital of the Narrative of Institution. The Elevation used took place before Communion, accompanied by the words τὰ ἅγια τοῖς ἁγίοις, "Holy things for holy people."

It is mentioned in S. Cyril's account and explained: "After this the priest says, 'Holy things for holy people.' Holy are the things which are lying on the altar through the reception of the overshadowing of the Holy Spirit. Holy are ye also, judged worthy of the gift of the Holy Spirit. Holy things therefore befit holy people." (Lat. version: S. P. opuscula, ed. Hurter, p. 128, and Migne, *P. G.* XXXIII. 1124.)

And S. Chrysostom refers to this usage and shows the meaning of it. It was a reminder of the need of holiness in the recipients of Holy things and a warning to the unholy not to draw near. "When the priest says, Holy things, etc., he says thus, If any man be not holy, let him not come here," etc. (S. Chrys. in Heb. c. x. Migne LXIII. c. 133.)

And S. James of Edessa in a letter of the 7th century on the Liturgy (Brightman, *Liturgies Eastern and Western*, Vol. I. pp. 490 f.) corroborates this view of the purpose of the words and act. "These holy things of the body and blood are given to the holy and pure, not to them that are not holy, and while he testifies this and cries aloud, he raises the Mysteries on high and shows them to all the people as if for a testimony, and the people immediately cry aloud and say, 'The one Father is holy,' and the rest. And so they communicate in the Mysteries."

This elevation with these words was general in the Eastern Liturgies. The Clementine does not expressly mention the act, though it has the words. This omission need not have great weight, as this was not a real Rite in use. It is expressly ordered in S. James[1], Syrian Jacobite[2], S. Basil[3], Armenian[4].

In the *Mozarabic Rite*[5] the two elevations are found. There is a twofold elevation during the Narrative of Institution, of the HOST following "This is My Body that is given for you," and of the CUP after "This... shed for you."

There is an elevation between the Canon and the Lord's Prayer, after the usual Eastern manner. The former evidently was dedicated Godward—presenting the gifts to GOD. The latter was directed—like the Eastern[6]—manward to inculcate faith and a right frame for the reception of the Sacrament, for it is followed[7] by the Nicene Creed and the Lord's Prayer.

"Dicat presbyter 'Fidem quam corde credimus, ore autem dicamus.'

"Et tunc elevet Sacerdos Corpus Christi, ut videatur a populo, et dicat chorus Symbolum" (Nicaenum).

---

[1] Brightman, *Liturgies Eastern and Western*, p. 61.

[2] *Ibid.* p. 101.   [3] *Ibid.* p. 341.   [4] *Ibid.* p. 447.

[5] *Missae Gothic. et Muzarabici Officii Expositio*, Lorenzana, pp. 42–4.

[6] The Eastern response was an expression of faith, e.g. S. James : εἷς ἅγιος, εἷς Κύριος, Ἰησοῦς Χριστός, εἰς δόξαν θεοῦ πατρός. Brightman, *Liturgies Eastern and Western*, Vol. I. p. 62.

S. Mark : εἷς πατὴρ ἅγιος, εἷς υἱὸς ἅγιος, ἓν πνεῦμα ἅγιον. *Ibid.* p. 138.

[7] Lorenzana, *op. cit.* p. 44.

The words "Sancta sanctis" are retained, but in a different connection, after the Lord's Prayer at the Commixture.

Sancta sanctis[1]: "Et conjunctio Corporis Domini nostri...sit sumentibus et potantibus nobis ad veniam," etc.

And then immediately the exhortation "Humiliate vos benedictioni...."

The Act of Elevation (after the Canon) and the Words, though divorced, both together have the old purport as an incentive to fitness to receive.

In the *Latin Rites* there is nothing exactly corresponding with the Eastern Elevation. There are three Elevations during the Canon, (1) at Qui Pridie, (2) at Simili Modo, (3) at Omnis honor et gloria.

The former two were probably in origin merely a solemn taking of the Elements to illustrate our Lord's action. There is no early evidence of their use.

There is in the 11th century a reference to them and an explanation on this line, viz.:

"Deinde panis in manus accipitur et ante quam reponatur in altare benedicitur: item et calix elevatus ante depositionem benedicitur. Nam et Dominus in evangelio utrumque legitur benedixisse antequam dimitteret e manibus. Accepta enim in manibus benedixit, postea discipulis dedit." (*Micrologus*, Cap. xv. De acceptione oblationis in manus.)

Archbishop Lorenzana (in his *Exposition of the*

---

[1] Lorenzana, *op. cit.* p. 47.

Mozarabic Office, p. 98) also admits their lateness, but hints at another reason:

" Before the times of the pestilent heresiarch Berengarius, the elevation of the Body and Blood of Christ was not made in the Roman Order before those words ' Est tibi...honor et gloria,' and similarly in the Mozarabic Office."

Probably the former explanation indicates an original and simpler elevation in imitation of what Christ did; the latter, a more pronounced elevation for a reverence to the Sacramental Presence—an outcome of the controversies of the time. Admittedly both were of late introduction.

The third elevation at " Omnis honor et gloria" is named in the Ordo Romanus[1] I. (*c.* A.D. 800), " Et dum venerit pontifex ad ' omnis honor et gloria,' *levat*," etc. This may well be the original elevation corresponding to the Eastern. Its purpose would seem to have been similar—to call out faith in Christ. Indeed it was connected by Ivo of Chartres[2] (12th century) with the Lord's words, " I, if I be lifted up, will draw all men unto me."

There is a *fourth elevation after* the Consecration.

" As soon as the words of Consecration are uttered, kneeling he adores the Consecrated Host; he rises, shows it to the people, replaces It on the Corporal, and adores It." (Roman rubric.)

And again—" raising himself as much as he well

---

[1] Duchesne, *Christian Worship*, p. 461.
[2] Ep. 231, Migne, *P. L.* CLXII. p. 234.

can, to lift up the Host on high and...reverently to show it to the people to be worshipped."

This is said to have arisen after the middle of the 11th century (Mabillon, *Comment. Praev. in Ord. Rom.*, Migne, *P.L.* LXXVIII. p. 877).

This is again admittedly not primitive and plainly for a purpose entirely different from that of the primitive elevation.

There is a *fifth elevation* introduced in the 16th century, before the Communion of the people, found first enjoined in the " Ritus celebrandi Missam " attached to the Pian Missal (1570).

"Tenet aliquantulum elevatum super pyxidem seu patinam et conversus ad communicandos in medio altaris dicit, 'Ecce Agnus Dei, ecce qui tollit peccata mundi.'"

This is in a similar place to the primitive elevation, before Communion and accompanied by an address to the Communicants. But the purpose is different—it is to call forth awe and worship and faith in Christ, but there is no reminder of the moral condition required in the Communicant. And it seems to localise the " Agnus Dei " too grossly. It is not used when there are no Communicants.

None of these elevations are primitive and none have the primitive purpose.

In our Liturgy, no Elevation is enjoined or provided for. But the purpose of the primitive Elevation of the Eastern Liturgies is served by our Invitation to the Communicants ("Ye that do truly...draw near with faith..."). That ancient Elevation was to remind men that holiness is needed for receiving "the Holy[1] Things." This is done with impressive solemnity in the " Invitation." And this effect would be greatly heightened, when this again occupies its right place, immediately before Communion.

II. *The Fraction.*

The Lord brake the one loaf for distribution after the " Words " had been said. This was the primitive purpose and significance of the Fraction. Later it came to be looked upon as symbolical of the Passion. S. Eutychius[2] says, " The fraction...shows the Sacrifice ($\sigma\phi\alpha\gamma\acute{\eta}\nu$)." And the Liturgy of the Syrian Jacobites at the Fraction makes the priest say, " Thus truly did the WORD of GOD suffer in the Flesh and was sacrificed and broken on the Cross[3]."

Hence the symbolical $\kappa\lambda\acute{\alpha}\sigma\iota\varsigma$ came to be distinct in some cases from the $\mu\epsilon\lambda\iota\sigma\mu\grave{o}\varsigma$ for distribution.

But any symbolical Fraction is not expressly mentioned before the 4th century, e.g. S. Cyril never refers to it and in his exposition it must have found a place had he known of it.

In the Clementine and Ethiopic there is no mention of any Fraction.

Serapion's Book[4] and S. Mark[5] have but one Fraction for distribution just before Communion.

[1] Cp. the definite application of this term to the Eucharist in the Didache, c. 9.
[2] Cited Brightman, *Liturgies Eastern and Western*, Vol. I. p. 533.
[3] *Ibid.* p. 97. [4] Edit. Wordsworth, S.P.C.K. p. 65.
[5] Brightman, *Liturgies Eastern and Western*, Vol. I. p. 138.

S. James[1] and the Nestorian[2] have it before Communion, partly for commixture and partly for distribution.

In Syrian Jacobite[3] and Armenian[4] there is the purely ceremonial Fraction for Commixture.

The old Byzantine[5] rites have the Fraction for distribution in the preparatory rite before the Mass, and no other, though the modern S. Chrysostom[5] has also a ceremonial Fraction before the Communion.

The Coptic[6] and Abyssinian[7] have it during the Narrative of Institution, but the former has a non-ceremonial Fraction also for distribution before the Lord's Prayer and Communion.

In the Western rites there was (in the MSS. preserved) only a ceremonial Fraction for purposes of " Commixture " before the Communion. The Gallican and Mozarabic interpose the Lord's Prayer between Fraction and Commixture. The Roman and Ambrosian make the Commixture follow on the Fraction immediately. The Fraction in the Mozarabic is of a more complicated character after the example of S. Chrysostom's Liturgy as now used. A similar manner prevailed in the Gallican rites too, for we find in an Irish Missal seven ways of Fraction provided, according to the nature of the day (Duchesne, *Christian Worship*, p. 220).

There are traces of a simpler ceremonial Fraction at the Narrative of Institution (after the manner of

[1] Brightman, *op. cit.* p. 62. [2] *Ibid.* p. 290 sq. [3] *Ibid.* p. 97.
[4] *Ibid.* p. 449. [5] Cp. *ibid.* pp. 341, 393, 539 sq.
[6] *Ibid.* pp. 177, 181. [7] *Ibid.* p. 232.

Coptic and Abyssinian). In the Sarum and York Missals (preserved in the late editions of 1555 and 1557) was a direction that at the word "fregit" the priest should touch (tangat) the Host, and in older copies "frangat hostiam" is actually found. And in a Missal of Rheims of the middle of the 16th century was the direction, "When he says He brake it, he breaks it a little."

Several other French Missals of the same period ordered a "show" of breaking at that point. (Scudamore, *Notit. Euch.* ed. I. p. 537.)

In the First Book of Edward VI. all ceremonial Fraction was omitted. But at the last Revision a ceremonial Fraction was reintroduced and placed at the Narrative of Institution, in imitation of the actual Institution. For any Fraction for purposes of distribution no provision was made.

As far as we can judge there was no Fraction in the earliest days, but for distribution. Later a ceremonial Fraction was introduced at a similar spot to the earlier Fraction, viz. just before Communion. But in the case of the Coptic and Abyssinian a ceremonial Fraction took place in illustration of the Narrative of Institution and of this traces are apparent in the West. And this simple symbolism our Office has adopted.

III. *Commixture.*

With the rise of the idea of the Fraction symbolising the Death of Christ, there arose a second idea of symbolising the Resurrection by dropping a particle of the Host into the chalice with appropriate words. It was accompanied in many rites by "Consignation," in which one species was signed by the other. In S. James[1] the signing followed, and in the Coptic[2], Nestorian[3] and Western rites preceded, the Commixture.

In the Byzantine[4] and Armenian[5] rites Commixture only is found. In the Syrian Jacobite[6] and Abyssinian[7] there is no separate form or act of Commixture, but only for Consignation. While in Bishop Serapion's Book[8], S. Mark[9], the Ethiopic[10] and the Clementine[11] there appears to be neither.

Both were omitted from the First Prayer Book of Edward VI., with the omission of the accompanying words. Both are absent from our present Office.

This omission can hardly be alleged as any defect in our Office. Undoubtedly these practices are of very early date, or else they would not have found place in the rites of sundered Jacobites and Nestorians or such general adoption.

Yet their absence from Serapion, S. Mark and the Ethiopic, from the Clementine and from S. Cyril's account testifies to their non-recognition in Egypt, Syria and Palestine in the 4th century. The testimony of the Clementine seems of peculiar value. It was

---

[1] Brightman, *Liturgies Eastern and Western*, Vol. i. p. 62.

[2] *Ibid.* p. 184.   [3] *Ibid.* p 291.

[4] *Ibid.* pp. 341, 394.   [5] *Ibid.* p. 449.

[6] *Ibid.* p. 97.   [7] *Ibid.* p. 240.

[8] Ed. Wordsworth, S.P.C.K. p. 65.

[9] Brightman, *op. cit.* p. 138.   [10] *Ibid.* p. 191.

[11] *Ibid.* pp. 24, 25.

supposed to represent the Liturgy of S. Clement of Rome and would represent the current and familiar use. A forgery designed to represent a real rite, it would hardly omit recognised features of the time and thus run the risk of detection.

As to the Manual Acts the general conclusion may well be that our Office, though without the Elevation, has an equivalent in the Invitation; that it has the Fraction in probably the original form and place; while the omission of Commixture and Consignation is but a reversion to primitive precedent.

ADDED NOTE. It may be argued that omission of the Fraction and Commixture of the old unreformed Office does not involve prohibition of them. But how can it be reasonably contended that acts are to continue to be done when the forms anciently accompanying them have been removed? And the rubrics in the Revised Book of 1549 definitely excluded them. After the Lord's Prayer, "*Then* shall the Priest say, 'The peace of the Lord be alway with you.' The clerks, 'And with thy spirit.' The Priest, 'Christ our Paschal Lamb,' etc. *Here* shall the Priest turn...and say, 'Ye that do truly repent,'" etc.

Where is room for the Fraction (after the Latin manner) and the Commixture? It is excluded.

COMPARISON OF THE ANGLICAN

Main features of General Eastern Type	Main features of Gallican Type	Main features of Roman Type
(1) Litany	(1) Litany [1]	(1) "Oremus"
(2) Offertory [Intercession : in Justin]	(2) Offertory (8) The Intercession	(2) Offertory ———
(3) Eucharistic Act ———	(3) Eucharistic Act ———	(3) Eucharistic Act (8) Part of Intercession
(4) Commemoration of Redemption	(4) Commemoration of Redemption	(7) Invocation
(5) and Narrative of Institution	(5) and Narrative of Institution	(5) Narrative of Institution
(6) Prayer of Oblation	(6) Prayer of Oblation	(6) Prayer of Oblation
(7) and Invocation	(7) and Invocation	———
(8) The Intercession	———	(8) and Rest of Intercession
———	(10) The Elevation and Fraction	———
(9) Communicants' Preparation: Lord's Prayer and Inclination	(9) Communicants' Preparation: Lord's Prayer [2] and Benediction	(9) Communicants' Preparation: Lord's Prayer
(10) Elevation and Manual Acts	———	(10) Manual Acts
		(9) Preparation of Communicants: 2 collects
(11) Communion	(11) Communion	(11) Communion
(12) Thanksgiving	(12) Thanksgiving	(12) Thanksgiving
(13) Prayer and Dismissal	(13) The Dismissal	(13) Dismissal

[1] In *Mozarabic* the Litany is absent.

[2] The Commixture came between the Lord's Prayer and Blessing in *Mozarabic*.

B

USE WITH ANCIENT STRUCTURES

1549	Present Office	American	Scottish
(2) Offertory	(2) Offertory	(2) Offertory	(2) Offertory
	(8) The Intercession	(8) The Intercession	
	(9) Part of Communicants' Preparation: Exhortation, Invitation, Confession, Absolution, and Comfortable Words	(9) Part of Communicants' Preparation: Exhortation, Invitation, Confession, Absolution, and Comfortable Words	
(3) Eucharistic Act	(3) Eucharistic Act	(3) Eucharistic Act	(3) Eucharistic Act
(8) The Intercession	(9) Part of Communicants' Preparation	(9) Part of Communicants' Preparation	
(4) ? Commemoration of Redemption	(4) ? Commemoration of Redemption	(4) Commemoration of Redemption	(4) Commemoration of Redemption
(7) Invocation	(7) Quasi-Invocation		
(5) Narrative of Institution	(5) Narrative of Institution	(5) Narrative of Institution	(5) Narrative of Institution
(6) Prayer of Oblation		(6) Prayer of Oblation	(6) Prayer of Oblation
	(11) Communion, and Lord's Prayer	(7) Invocation and Rest of Prayer of Oblation	(7) Invocation and Rest of Prayer of Oblation
	(6) Prayer of Oblation		(8) The Intercession
(9) Communicants' Preparation: Lord's Prayer, Salutation, Invitation, Confession, Absolution, Comfortable Words and Prayer of "Humble Access"			(9) Communicants' Preparation: Lord's Prayer, Salutation, Invitation, Confession, Absolution, Comfortable Words and Prayer of "Humble Access"
(11) Communion		(11) Communion, and Lord's Prayer	(11) Communion
(12) Thanksgiving	(12) Thanksgiving and Gloria	(12) Thanksgiving and Gloria	(12) Thanksgiving and Gloria
(13) The Blessing	(13) The Blessing	(13) The Blessing	(13) The Blessing

APPENDIX C

COMPARISON OF THE COMPOSITION OF OUR PRESENT CANON WITH THE CANON OF 1549 AND THAT OF THE SARUM OFFICE.

N.B.   Italic type represents common matter.

Sarum	Prayer Book of 1549	Present Office
1. *The Lord be with you.* *And with thy spirit.* *Lift up your hearts.* *We lift them up unto the Lord.* *Let us give thanks unto our Lord God.* *It is meet and right so to do.*	1. *The Lord be with you.* *And with thy spirit.* *Lift up your hearts.* *We lift them up unto the Lord.* *Let us give thanks unto our Lord God.* *It is meet and right so to do.*	*Lift up your hearts.* *We lift them up unto the Lord.* *Let us give thanks unto our Lord God.* *It is meet and right so to do.*
2. *It is very meet, right,* fitting and profitable, *that we should at all times, and in all places, give thanks unto thee, O* holy *Lord, Almighty Father, everlasting God: And therefore with Angels and Archangels,* with thrones and dominions, *and with every company of the heavenly host,* we sing the hymn of thy *Glory, saying evermore:—*	*It is very meet, right,* and our bounden duty, *that we should at all times and in all places, give thanks unto thee, O Lord,* holy *Father, Almighty, everlasting God: Therefore with Angels and Archangels, and all the* holy *company of heaven,* we laud and magnify thy *Glorious* Name, *evermore* praising thee and *saying:*	*It is very meet, right,* and our bounden duty, *that we should at all times, and in all places, give thanks unto thee, O Lord,* holy *Father, Almighty, everlasting God: Therefore with Angels and Archangels, and all the company of heaven,* we laud and magnify thy *Glorious* Name, *evermore* praising thee and *saying:*
3. *Holy, Holy, Holy, Lord God of Hosts, Heaven and earth are full of thy glory:* *Hosanna in the highest:*	3. *Holy, Holy, Holy, Lord God of Hosts, Heaven and earth are full of thy glory :* *Hosanna in the highest:*	3. *Holy, Holy, Holy, Lord God of Hosts, Heaven and earth are full of thy glory :* Glory be to thee, O Lord Most High.
Blessed is he that cometh in the Name of the Lord : *Hosanna in the highest.*	*Blessed is he that cometh in the Name of the Lord :* *Hosanna in the highest.* Blessed is he that cometh in the Name of the Lord; Glory to thee, O Lord, in the highest.	

Sarum	Prayer Book of 1549	Present Office
	Let us pray for the whole state of Christ's Church.	Let us pray for the whole state of Christ's Church + (militant here in earth.)
4. Therefore, most merciful Father, through Jesus Christ, thy Son, our Lord,	Almighty and ever-living God, who by thy Holy Apostle hast taught us to make prayers and supplications and to give thanks for all men;	Almighty and ever-living God, who by thy Holy Apostle hast taught us to make prayers and supplications and to give thanks for all men;
we humbly pray and *beseech thee to receive these* gifts, these offerings, these holy undefiled sacrifices, *which* first of all, *we offer to thee,* for thy Holy *Catholic Church,* which do thou vouchsafe to keep in peace, to watch over, to *unite* and govern throughout the whole world[1];	*we humbly beseech thee,* most mercifully *to receive these* our prayers *which we offer* unto thy Divine Majesty, beseeching thee to inspire continually the *universal Church,* with the spirit of truth, *unity* and concord; and grant that all they that do confess thy holy Name, may agree in the truth of thy holy Word, and live in *unity* and godly love[1];	*we humbly beseech thee* most mercifully to accept our alms and oblations, and *to receive these* our prayers *which we offer* unto thy Divine Majesty, beseeching thee to inspire continually the *universal Church,* with the spirit of truth, *unity* and concord; and grant that all they that do confess thy holy Name, may agree in the truth of thy holy Word, and live in *unity* and godly love[1];
together with *thy servant* [our Pope, and our Bishop, N. and] *our King, N,*	Specially we beseech thee to save and defend *thy servant, Edward, our King,* that under him we may be godly and quietly governed; and grant unto his whole council, and to all that are put in authority under him, that they may truly and indifferently minister justice, to the punishment of wickedness and vice, and to the maintenance of thy true religion and virtue.	We beseech thee also to save and defend *thy servant, George, our King,* that under him we may be godly and quietly governed; and grant unto his whole council, and to all that are put in authority under him, that they may truly and indifferently minister justice, to the punishment of wickedness and vice, and to the maintenance of thy true religion and virtue.

[1] Similarity of idea.

Sarum	Prayer Book of 1549	Present Office
[*our Bishop, N.*]	Give grace, O heavenly Father, to *all Bishops,* Pastors and Curates, that they may both by their life and doctrine set forth thy true and lively Word, and rightly and duly administer thy holy Sacraments.	Give grace, O heavenly Father, to *all Bishops* and Curates, that they may both by their life and doctrine set forth thy true and lively Word, and rightly and duly administer thy holy Sacraments.
and all right believers and maintainers of the Catholic and Apostolic Faith[1]. *Remember, O Lord, thy servants and handmaidens N. and N. and all here standing around...*	And to all thy people, give thy heavenly grace that, with meek heart and due reverence, they may hear, and receive thy holy Word; truly serving thee in holiness and righteousness all the days of their life[1]. And we most humbly beseech thee of thy goodness, O Lord, to comfort and succour all them, who in this transitory life are in trouble, sorrow, need, sickness or any other adversity.	And to all thy people, give thy heavenly grace, and specially *to this congregation here present,* that with meek heart and due reverence, they may hear, and receive thy holy Word; truly serving thee in holiness and righteousness all the days of their life[1]. And we most humbly beseech thee of thy goodness, O Lord, to comfort and succour all them, who in this transitory life are in trouble, sorrow, need, sickness or any other adversity.
whose faith is known, and devotion noted by thee, for whom we offer unto thee, or who are offering unto thee this *sacrifice of praise*[2] for themselves and all theirs, for the redemption of their souls, for the hope of salvation and safety, and who unto thee are paying their vows, O everlasting God, living and true.	*And especially we commend unto thy merciful goodness, this congregation which is here assembled in* thy Name to celebrate the commemoration of the most glorious death of thy son :	

---

[1] Similarity of idea.

[2] Later in our English Offices in Prayer of Oblation.

Sarum	Prayer Book of 1549	Present Office
In communion with, and ever venerating the memory *firstly of the glorious and ever Virgin Mary, mother of Jesus Christ, our Lord and God, and* also of thy blessed *Apostles and Martyrs,* Peter, N.N. *and of all thy saints,*	And here we do give unto thee most high praise and hearty thanks for the wonderful grace and virtue declared in *all thy saints from the beginning of the world, and chiefly in the glorious* and most blessed *Virgin Mary, mother of thy son Jesus Christ, our Lord and God, and in* the Holy Patriarchs, Prophets, *Apostles and Martyrs,*	And we also bless thy holy Name for all thy *servants* departed this life in thy *faith* and fear;
by whose merits and prayers grant that we may in all things be defended by the help of thy protection through the same Jesus Christ our Lord. Amen.	whose examples, O Lord, stedfastness in thy faith and keeping thy holy commandments grant us to follow.	beseeching thee to give us grace so to follow their good examples,
[8. After Consecration. Remember, O Lord, the souls of thy *servants* and handmaidens, N. and N., who have gone before us *with the sign of faith, and repose in the sleep of peace; grant unto them, we beseech thee, O Lord,* and to all that rest in Christ, a place of refreshment, light and *peace:* through the same Jesus Christ, our Lord. Amen.]	We commend unto thy mercy, O Lord, all other thy *servants* which departed hence from *us with the sign of faith, and now do rest in the sleep of peace. Grant unto them, we beseech thee,* thy mercy and everlasting *peace:* and that at the day of the general resurrection, we and all they which be of the mystical body of thy son, may altogether be set on thy right hand, and hear His most joyful voice: "Come, ye blessed of My Father, inherit	that with them

Sarum	Prayer Book of 1549	Present Office
	the kingdom prepared for you from the beginning of the world. Grant this, O Father, for Jesus Christ's sake, our only Mediator and Advocate.	we may be partakers of thy heavenly kingdom. Grant this, O Father, for Jesus Christ's sake, our only Mediator and Advocate. Amen.
5. *This oblation*[1], therefore, *of our service* as also of thy whole household, *we beseech thee,* favourably *to accept,* O Lord, and to order our days in thy peace, and command that we be delivered from eternal damnation, and numbered with the flock of thine elect through Jesus Christ our Lord.		
	O God, Heavenly Father, who of thy tender mercy didst give thy only Son Jesus Christ to suffer death upon the cross for our redemption; who made there, (by his one oblation of himself once offered) a full, perfect and sufficient sacrifice, oblation and satisfaction, for the sins of the whole world, and did institute, and in his holy Gospel command us to celebrate, a perpetual memory of that his precious death until his coming again :	Almighty God, our Heavenly Father, who of thy tender mercy didst give thy only Son Jesus Christ to suffer death upon the cross for our redemption; who made there, (by his one oblation of himself once offered) a full, perfect and sufficient sacrifice, oblation and satisfaction, for the sins of the whole world, and did institute, and in his holy Gospel command us to continue, a perpetual memory of that his precious death until his coming again :
Which oblation, we beseech thee, Almighty God, do thou *vouchsafe altogether to render blessed,*	Hear us, O merciful Father, we beseech Thee, and with thy Word and Holy Spirit *vouchsafe to*	Hear us, O merciful Father, we most humbly beseech thee and grant that we receiving these

[1] Oblationem servitutis nostrae, reproduced in English Prayer of Oblation.

Sarum	Prayer Book of 1549	Present Office
approved, ratified, reasonable and acceptable, *that it may be made unto us the Body and Blood of thy most dearly beloved Son, our Lord Jesus Christ, who,* on the day before He suffered, *took Bread* into His Holy and venerable Hands and with His eyes uplifted towards Heaven unto thee, O God, His Almighty Father, *giving thanks to thee, He blessed, brake it, and gave it to His disciples, saying, Take and eat ye all of this, for this is my Body.*	*bless and sanctify,* these thy creatures of Bread and Wine, that they may be *unto us the Body and Blood of thy most dearly beloved Son, our Lord Jesus Christ, who,* in the same night that he was betrayed, *took Bread,*	thy creatures of Bread and Wine, according to thy Son, our Saviour, Jesus Christ's holy institution, in remembrance of his death and passion, may be partakers of his most blessed *Body and Blood, who* in the same night that he was betrayed, *took bread*
Likewise, after supper taking also this excellent *Cup* into His Holy and venerable Hands, again *giving thanks* unto thee, He blessed It, and *gave it to* His disciples, *saying, Drink ye all of this, for this is* the Cup of *My Blood of the New* and everlasting *Testament,* the mystery of Faith, which shall be *shed for you and for many for remission of sins: as often as ye do these things ye shall do them in remembrance of me.*	*and when He had blessed and given thanks, He brake and gave it to His disciples, saying, Take, eat, this is My Body, which is given* for you, Do this in remembrance of me; *Likewise after supper, He took the Cup, and when He had given thanks, He gave it to* them, *saying, Drink ye all of this, for this is My Blood of the New Testament,* which is *shed for you and for many, for remission of sins: Do this as oft as ye shall drink it, in remembrance of me.*	*and when he had given thanks, he brake and gave it to his disciples, saying, Take, eat, this is my Body, which is given* for you, Do this in remembrance of me; *Likewise after supper, he took the Cup, and when he had given thanks, he gave it to* them, *saying, Drink ye all of this, for this is my Blood of the New Testament,* which is *shed for you and for many, for remission of sins: Do this as oft as ye shall drink it, in remembrance of me.*
7. *Wherefore also, O Lord, we thy servants* but also thy holy people,	*Wherefore, O Lord* and Heavenly Father, according to the Institution of thy dearly be-	*O Lord* and Heavenly Father,

Sarum	Prayer Book of 1549	Present Office
	loved Son, our Saviour Jesus Christ, *we, thy* humble *servants*, do celebrate and make here before *thy* Divine *Majesty with thy holy gifts*, the memorial which thy Son hath willed so to make,	we *thy* humble *servants*,
having in remembrance the so blessed passion of the same thy Son, Jesus Christ, our Lord, as also His Resurrection from the dead, and also His glorious Ascension into the Heavens, do offer to *thy* excellent *Majesty of thy gifts* and bounties, a pure offering, a holy offering, an undefiled offering, the holy Bread of eternal life, and the cup of everlasting salvation, upon which do thou vouchsafe to look with favour and gracious countenance, and hold them accepted, as thou didst vouchsafe in the presents of thy servant Abel, and the sacrifice of our forefather Abraham and that holy sacrifice the pure offering which thy High Priest Melchizedek did offer to thee,	*having in remembrance His blessed Passion,* mighty *Resurrection and glorious Ascension,*	
	rendering to thee most hearty thanks for the innumerable benefits procured to us by the same, entirely desiring thy fatherly goodness mercifully to accept *this our*	entirely desire thy fatherly goodness mercifully to accept *this our*

Sarum	Prayer Book of 1549	Present Office
	Sacrifice of praise[1] and thanksgiving: most humbly beseeching thee to grant that by the merits and death of thy Son, Jesus Christ, and through faith in His blood, we and all thy whole Church may obtain remission of our sins, and all other benefits of His passion.	*Sacrifice of praise*[1] and thanksgiving; most humbly beseeching thee to grant that by the merits and death of thy Son, Jesus Christ, and through faith in His blood, we and all thy whole Church may obtain remission of our sins, and all other benefits of His passion.
	And here we offer and present unto thee, O Lord, ourselves, our souls and bodies, to be a reasonable, holy and lively sacrifice unto thee:	And here we offer and present unto thee, O Lord, ourselves, our souls and bodies, to be a reasonable, holy and lively sacrifice unto thee:
that as many of us, as by this *partaking* of the Altar *shall have received the most* sacred *Body and Blood of thy Son, may be fulfilled with all heavenly benediction and grace, through Jesus Christ our Lord. Amen.*	*humbly beseeching thee, that whosoever shall be partakers of this* Holy Communion may worthily *receive the most* precious *Body and Blood of thy Son, Jesus Christ, and be fulfilled with thy grace and heavenly benediction,* and be made one Body with thy Son, Jesus Christ, that He may dwell in them and they in Him. And although we be unworthy, through our manifold sins, to offer unto thee any *sacrifice, yet we beseech thee to accept this, our bounden duty and service*[2]; *and command these* our prayers and supplications, *by the ministry of thy Holy Angels to be brought up into thy Holy*	*humbly beseeching thee* that all we who are *partakers* of this Holy Communion *may be fulfilled with thy grace and heavenly benediction.* And although we be unworthy, through our manifold sins, to offer unto thee any *sacrifice, yet we beseech thee to accept this, our bounden duty and service*[2]:
We humbly beseech thee, Almighty God, *command these things to be brought up by the hands of thy Holy Angel,* to thy Altar		

[1] See above (4) in Sarum.
[2] Represents oblationem servitutis nostrae in "Hanc oblationem," no. 5.

Sarum	Prayer Book of 1549	Present Office
on High, *before the sight of thy Divine Majesty :*	*Tabernacle, before the sight of thy Divine Majesty :*	
8. *Memento.* Remember etc. (vide supra).		
9*. Unto us sinners, also, thy servants that hope in the multitude of thy mercies, vouchsafe to grant some part of fellowship with thy Holy Apostles, and Martyrs, N. N. and all thy Saints; unto whose company do thou admit us :		
not weighing our merits, but bestowing pardon, we beseech thee, through Christ our Lord; through whom, O Lord, all these good gifts thou dost ever create, sanctify, quicken, bless and bestow upon us.	*not weighing our merits* but *pardoning* our offences, *through Jesus Christ our Lord;*	*not weighing our merits* but *pardoning* our offences, *through Jesus Christ our Lord;*
By Him and with Him, and in Him, *in the unity of the Holy Ghost, all honour and glory* is *unto thee,* God the *Father Almighty, world without end. Amen.* *Let us pray.*	*By* whom and *with* whom *in the unity of the Holy Ghost, all honour and glory* be *unto thee,* O *Father Almighty, world without end. Amen.* *Let us pray.*	*By* whom and *with* whom *in the unity of the Holy Ghost, all honour and glory* be *unto thee,* O *Father Almighty, world without end. Amen.*
10. Admonished by salutary *commands, and* directed by Divine *teaching, we are bold to say :* "*Our Father............* ......*But deliver us from evil. Amen.*"	As our Saviour Christ hath *commanded and taught us, we are bold to say :* "*Our Father............* ....*evil. Amen.*"	

* A repetition of § 4.

Sarum	Prayer Book of 1549	Present Office
11. Deliver us, we beseech thee, O Lord, from all evils, past, present and future, and at the intercession of Mary, glorious and ever Virgin and all thy saints, graciously give peace in our time, that aided by the succour of thy mercy, we may be both free evermore from sin, and secure from all alarm; through Jesus Christ our Lord, who liveth and reigneth with thee, and the Holy Ghost, one God, world without end. Amen. *The peace of the Lord be always with you.* *And with thy spirit.* [*The Agnus, Commixture and the Kiss of Peace.*]	} Do. Christ, our paschal Lamb, is offered up for us once for all, when He bare our sins in His Body on the Cross, for He is the very Lamb of God, that taketh away the sins of the world; wherefore let us keep the feast joyful and holy with the Lord. *Nota bene. Rubric.* *Here* the Priest shall turn and say, "Ye that do Truly" (excluding Commixture and Elevation).	

INDEX

For EU product safety concerns, contact us at Calle de José Abascal, 56–1°,
28003 Madrid, Spain or eugpsr@cambridge.org.